ESPRIT DE CORPSE

"I'm gonna be a policeman, just like you, dad!"

THOMAS CAVERLY

◆ FriesenPress

Suite 300 - 990 Fort St
Victoria, BC, V8V 3K2
Canada

www.friesenpress.com

This book is dedicated to my fellow brother and sister law enforcement officers, but more so to my wife, Janette, family and friends who helped me to survive a career in law enforcement.

Special thanks to my colleagues below who took their time to read my book and gave their insights that, in the end, contributed to this book:

Bob Page (Insp. Ret) Supt. Murray Power, Marion Craig (Sgt. Ret), Det. Ian Parks, Insp. Colin Thompson and Sgt. Mike Wheeler.

Members of the RCMP, Abbotsford Police Service and Vancouver Police Department

ISBN
978-1-5255-0889-9 (Hardcover)
978-1-5255-0890-5 (Paperback)
978-1-5255-0891-2 (eBook)

1. SELF-HELP, MOTIVATIONAL & INSPIRATIONAL

Distributed to the trade by The Ingram Book Company

Cover Concept

Esprit de Corps is a common spirit amongst group members that inspires enthusiasm, devotion and a strong sense of honour. It is entrenched deeply in the RCMP's history based on traditions, and it is the thread that binds their members together. This spirit may change over time, and each generation will live it in its own way. It is like the phoenix that continues to rise from the ashes, never really dying but rather reinventing itself. It is this spirit that remains a constant in this hallmark institution of Canada. When I explained esprit de corps to the artist Justin Longoz, it inspired him to create this image.

"The police are the public and the public are the police; the police being only members of the public who are paid to give full time attention to duties which are incumbent on every citizen in the interests of community welfare and existence."

—Sir Robert Peel, Father of modern policing,
Principles of Law Enforcement, 1829

Sukh,

Thanks for your service!
It is appreciated. Take time,
now and again, to reflect on
the good times of your career.
I hope my words help
get you there.

Westerly

TABLE OF CONTENTS

PREFACE

The inspiration for this book grew over twenty-seven years of policing and took another three years to move from a concept to paper. It is meant for those police officers who want to maintain tradition and, in the case of the RCMP, restore tradition and reputation. It sets the stage for success in policing and guidance on how to leave a positive legacy – a legacy meant for generations to come with a true understanding of what it means to maintain the right.

INTRODUCTION

The leader of the band is tired
And his eyes are growing old
But his blood runs through my instrument
And his song is in my soul.

"Leader of the Band"
—Dan Fogelberg, 1981

In a world that's always turned upside down, we all want a sense that everything is going to be just fine – even more so, when you are talking about your country. To Canada, the RCMP is the nation's protector, standing for family, kinship, and pride. It is born out of tradition and is etched in stone of our culture, recognized as a worldwide icon. *Esprit de corps* is what etched it into stone, and it can never be taken for granted. It is every generation's obligation to dig down deep, reflect upon it, and find its own personal meaning and collective practice of esprit de corps. To fail in this obligation means to fail a country. To fail in this obligation means esprit de *corpse*.

The RCMP has always meant family to me, but like any other family, it sometimes loses its way or even becomes dysfunctional. When a family is in this state, it is up to its members to fight for it in order to keep it alive. Esprit de corps is the torch that is handed down from one generation to the next. It is the key that makes a difference. The degree of difference will depend on the previous generation's ability to provide a legacy that demonstrates forward thinking, perseverance, and loyalty. It is always a matter of surviving the test of time and knowing where and what we want to be, which translates to being in a better place than before.

It begins at the individual level with the ability to see that each of us cannot do it alone, realizing that we must seek help along the way. Guidance has always been helpful in this regard. It has always been there for the taking, and it manifests itself in many forms. It can be by surprise or by design. Mine was initially in the form of a personal rather than a professional relationship. It was a father/son relationship that would later transform into my career as a member of our nation's police force. My father dedicated twenty-three years of his life to the Force (synonymous with the RCMP), and he was my inspiration to join. At the time, I really did not appreciate the importance of the day of my graduation from "Depot Division". My father presented me with my badge, but it was more about that *torch* being passed to me. It was a dream come true and a privilege to be part of an important part of our history. More importantly, it also meant an obligation to serve my country.

This history is not without blood, sweat, and tears. Many have sacrificed and have been successful in building on the RCMP's history. Success is a funny thing, as it means different things to different people. It can come from financial gain, job satisfaction, a healthy family, or in an altruistic sense, it can mean that you are making a difference in people's lives. *Whatever* you decide is important should become the catalyst to create a plan for your success. Listen to all that you can, and take what you feel is worth keeping for your own personal plan.

Always start with an end in mind and, no matter what stage you are at in your life, consider these questions: "Where do I want to go in my career, and how will I get there? How will I survive dealing with the worst of the worst or seeing the worst of the worst and still be able to have some sense of normality?" Of course, the most important question will be "When do I retire?" You will never be alone in your policing journey as there will be many who will give you a hand along the way. Never be afraid to ask them for help. They are expecting it and will likely welcome your request, just as people were there for them over the course of *their* journey.

Police work is not an easy profession.

Through thick and thin, family will always be there for you during your law enforcement career. They help to keep you real and grounded with emotional support. Never forget that, at times, it will be just as much a challenge for them in dealing with the effects of this demanding line of work. As much as you try to impress upon them what it is to live with a cop, each individual is affected differently. Realizing this means you need to constantly work on your relationships to keep them alive and healthy. The main point is that, in the end, you want to walk out the door with as few scars as possible so that you can enjoy your retirement years with the ones you love.

It is a gross understatement when I say that police work is not an easy profession. It is the ultimate journey, and occasionally, it involves the ultimate sacrifice. It will have numerous bumps along the way and will bring with it the fear of the unknown. It never seems to make sense that we all have to hit the same bumps over and over again or deal with that same unknown. The pages within the cover of this book are meant to assist with this, but more than that, they are meant to challenge you to be more than you ever imagined you could be. I hope that the words that follow will give you that self-help, that motivation, that how-to impulse, and finally, a sense of direction. This, along with a simple message: regardless of the profession we have chosen, we need to develop the ability to laugh at the situation and, more importantly, at ourselves.

Music can serve to motivate us, relax us, or bring back memories, both happy and sad. Songs and their lyrics always say so much, and their impact varies greatly from individual to individual. Not unlike taking the time to smell the flowers, it is advisable to stop and listen to what the music is saying to us. Tunes and lyrics also help us to find solace when needed. It does not matter what the topic is, you can almost always find a song that fits the situation perfectly. Reflect on the lyrics at the beginning of each chapter and ask yourself what the words mean to you.

Police work requires knowledge of the law, knowing when to lead, when to follow, when to listen, but ultimately, it is ninety-five percent common sense. You can read endless books on these subjects but, in the end, it is irrelevant unless you can make meaning of those words and then apply them to your work as a police officer. With this in mind, this book is written from a practical perspective, aimed at best practices to get the job done. It touches on the roots of the RCMP and moves on to broader topics designed to give practical advice that will provide a framework for success in policing.

Chapter One
PLAN YOUR RETIREMENT
STARTING ON DAY ONE

You think you have time
You think tomorrow's always coming down the line
And then one day
You wake up and you find
The trouble is you thought you had time.

"Time"
—Dean Brody, 2016

It was a few months before I retired, and Paul was in town to facilitate a course in which I had played a role over the years. It was a quiet Sunday morning, and we sat on the front porch getting caught up on one another's news. Paul is one of those guys who is not only a true friend, but also a good listener. During a phone call, I had spoken to him about a job outside the RCMP, recognizing it would mean leaving a job I loved so much. I was relatively quiet during this particular conversation, and the topic of what I was going to do next came up. It was as if I was trying very hard to convince him that the particular job on my horizon was a great opportunity. Actually, the truth was that the job was going to be far from challenging for me, but this was not the main point. It was more of a self-realization that I could not keep doing what I was doing at the same frantic pace, while still maintaining any kind of life/work balance. Paul just looked at me and said, "You're done." It was not even posed as a question, it

1

was a statement. I looked at him and finally replied, "Yes, I am done." It struck me that Paul had said something out loud that I should have said myself long before our conversation. The fact that I had not been able to meant that I was in a state of denial, unable to face the inevitable.

One morning, you wake up and you know that it is finally time to leave. Everyone has their own personal reasons for leaving, and each person has to make the decision on their own terms. You do not want to be in a position where you feel like you are being forced to retire or with the sense that your contribution is not as stellar as it once was. We claim to know that we will all get there one day but, at the same time, we manage to kid ourselves by saying, "It will never happen to me." As strange as it sounds, you need to plan for this day even before you start Day One of your career and never lose sight of your "Date."

As any good financial planner will tell you, map your retirement well in advance so that you can live life the way you want to live it. This mapping is based on what is important to you on a number of fronts – financial, lifestyle, health. Let's just assume you're one of the lucky ones, and your career path leads you to one of those jobs you can't wait to get out of bed to do, and by the end, you have achieved everything that you set out to accomplish. This is what happened to me, and even on my last day as a Mountie, I had just as much passion for the job as I had on my very first day. The only difference between those two bookends of my career was that, on my last day, I was able to reflect on what I had done, where I had been, and I was able to count the ways I contributed to the RCMP's mandate over the years. In short, I felt a great sense of accomplishment. This realization, coupled with the understanding that it was never going to be easy to leave, whether it was one year, two years, or even ten years down the road, helped me to finally make my decision.

Determine Your "Best Before Dates"

Beyond the obvious considerations, I wondered why making the decision was so difficult, and I eventually determined that it was the fear of such a major change and the prospect of leaving the organization that had won my lifelong loyalty. Like any lifelong commitment, the thought of leaving caused a great deal of stress and angst. I overheard a conversation with three non-commissioned officers (NCOs), and of course, the topic was the number of detachment retirements and how individuals come to grips with making that decision. I listened and added what I believed was the RCMP specific challenge – namely that we simply do not know how to quit. I was speaking specifically about my generation, the Baby Boomers, because experts are now suggesting that individuals will have at least eight careers in their lifetime and that organizational loyalty will no longer be lifelong. The three NCOs looked at me and agreed, at least, in principle.

The reason why we have trouble realizing that it is time to move on stems from the fact that we do not listen to ourselves and readily accept our "Best Before Date." This is an important term in the context of knowing when

When we do finally act, it feels as if the weight of the world has been taken off our shoulders.

you should consider changing jobs or retiring. Many of us know when we have reached our best before date, but for one reason or another, we fail to take the next step. For the most part, this inability to act is based on fear and/or the unwillingness to change. What is most important to realize is that when we do finally act, it feels as if the weight of the world has been taken off our shoulders.

How do you know when you have reached this point? During your career, you will not necessarily stay on a straight path. You may explore various aspects of policing, some of which may be more appealing to you than others. During my time with the RCMP, I bounced back and forth from plainclothes duties to uniform duties. As a result, I encountered several best before dates. Often, you intuitively know when you need a change or need to take a step that will assist your career advancement. It could also be that that your present assignment is interfering with your life/work balance (LWB) or it is simply no longer offering you the opportunity to grow. Establish criteria to help you decide what your best before dates will be and use those as career milestones to get you to where you want to be.

The last milestone will be retirement. As illustrious as his career was, even the Great Gretzky struggled with his best before date. Rob Vollman, author of

Rob Vollman's Hockey Abstract and co-author of the annual *Hockey Prospectus Guides,* wrote an article questioning whether the Great One had retired too early. He begins by reflecting on Gretzky's accomplishments. He cites Wayne Gretzky as the greatest hockey player of all time, retired at age thirty-eight, right before the conclusion of the 1998–99 NHL season. Having led the league in assists two of the past three seasons and having led the Rangers in scoring for the third straight season, he certainly retired when he was on top. In his article, he explored the reasons Gretzky likely considered in making his tough decision. Vollman questioned whether they were physical, personal, or as he suggested in his retirement announcement, simply a gut feeling. What is interesting about this article is that it demonstrates that, no matter who you are or what you have accomplished, you will still experience the same struggles in determining that best before date. What is clear is that Wayne Gretzky had an idea of what that date was, and he prepared himself to make that tough decision. Just know that when it comes time for your decision it is always "fifty-fifty, call a friend" but it has to be right for you.

> **Often, you intuitively know when you need a change or you need to take a step that will assist you career advancement.**

I think that part of the challenge around this is somehow associated with our insecurities and for the same reasons midlife crises occur. We want to know what we've accomplished in life and that we have somehow left our mark. When you are at the point where you're deciding to leave or not, you have to ask yourself these questions: Is our fear that we have not done anything worthy of note and, therefore, left no mark? Could it be that our egos are not strong enough to handle this? This always reminds me of something that was shown to me when I was posted in Valleyview, Alberta. I was quite junior in service, with only a few years' experience, and one of the senior constables was being transferred out. He took me to his workstation and shared a story with me, the theme being the lasting impact of our efforts.

In this story, a man was asked to take a full glass of water, place his finger in it and then spin it around. You can picture this, you can see the little water tornado forming. This was a reflection of the influence you had during your time in this workplace. The man was then told to take his finger out of the water, and a short time later, the water was again still. The water went back to its original state, implying that all the hard work this man had done really meant nothing. Even though I was inexperienced, I could neither believe nor accept this explanation. No matter what profession you choose, you will have left a mark, either through your work on files and initiatives or through the relationships you built while you were there. I chose not to subscribe to the moral of this story, and I would encourage you not to either. In fact, the belief of not having made a difference actually goes against the grain as to why people choose law enforcement as a practice in the first place. After being told this story, I personally committed even more to making a difference wherever my work journey took me. I can rest easy, knowing that I have had an impact and made a lasting difference, particularly in the relationships I forged along the way.

In a perfect world, you will accomplish what you set out to do in your career, while managing to keep your health intact regardless of whether you have a desk job or are responding to calls for service. It also means sound financial planning so that you truly can enjoy the rest of your life. You won't get an argument from your family on this because this practice will have taken enough of your precious time from your family, and if you have done it right, they will want to get it back. I remember hearing my mom say a couple of times after my dad retired from the Force that it was now her turn. I never really quite appreciated that at the time, but I do now. Your choice to retire affects all the loved ones in your life. I found this poem that you should consider when you get wrapped up in yourself about this life-changing decision. Although reference is made to a wife in this poem, the sentiment is really directed to any partner who has the challenge of living with a police officer.

Thomas Caverly

"A Police Officer's Wife"

A special kind of woman: a cut above the rest,
That's a Police Officer's Wife, rating her best.

How many goodbyes are whispered, joined with a fond embrace?
As duty steals her man, for the danger he must face.

How often have meals been ruined – or tender moments disturbed,
by a call for special duty, sparking loyalty unswerved?

It's a devil of a job, for an angel like this,
Who for the love of her man, must forsake that kiss.

She can run a garden tractor; even paint a room in need,
How she can stretch a dollar is a miracle indeed.

She's mother, lover, chauffeur and nurse,
A living symbol of: "for better or for worse."

Rich is the man, reaping his rewards in life,
Who chose to be the other half of

—Author Unknown

Your world will not focus around police work and hopefully you will have
both arrived at your destination's oasis or have a different focus. This is what life
is really all about, finishing together. The goal is to retire without becoming an
alcoholic or suffering from depression.

When you come to the point where you make the decision and take that
plunge off the edge of the cliff into retirement, know that there is no going
back. There may be some *buyer's remorse*; after all, you just bought retirement,
but steer away from regretting your decision. Regrets will take the joy out of the

new life you have just started to embrace. Keep in mind that you have reached the point in life that so many others aspire to. You have either *survived* or *made it,* and now you deserve to enjoy every moment of this new adventure.

August 2014 was the perfect time for me to leave, for I knew that I would be leaving at the top of my game – a well-respected member who had earned many accolades and was able to sit back and reflect on a successful career. I was then asked what I was going to do when I was no longer a cop. I looked at this individual and stated emphatically that I would always be a Mountie. I grew up with a dad who was a Mountie, and I knew that I would be a Mountie for life, without any question. However, this was not the real question.

Remember Role Theory

During my first year of college, I remember learning about role theory. Without constructing a thesis paper, I will tell you what I understood and what I learned from that first class. This theory subscribes to the premise that we are different people, in different roles, and that will result in us demonstrating different behaviours. This was easy to understand as it made sense that there are certain expectations of people when they are in a specific role. As an example, if I was in charge of an RCMP plainclothes unit, I would be expected to be well-organized, have a strong personality, act professionally at all times, and walk with an air of confidence. Think about what your expectations are of doctors, lawyers, judges, and teachers. I could go on but I believe I've made the point.

What I took away from that class was that, when you walked into one of those demanding roles, somehow who you were as a person got lost. This is why, when asked the question "Who am I", most people respond by referring to one of their roles, for instance, "I am a mother, I am a student ..." Answers like these do not get at the heart of who we really are. This was the real question that was being asked of me. After that first class, I promised myself that, no matter what role I was going to assume, I was going to let people see the person behind that role. This did not mean that I would disregard the expectations associated with the role of S/Sgt Caverly, but I would also ensure that people were able to see the man who was Tom. I still received the respect due my rank, but more importantly, I also received the respect for the man *behind* the rank, making it so much easier to interact with people at all levels in the pursuit and achievement of common goals.

I believe that this approach was, and is, one of the reasons that helped my transition from a police officer to a civilian. Oh, and upon further thought, since role theory also allows us to fulfill several roles at any one time, I guess that I was always a civilian!

The Real Meaning of Transition

This brings me to my next point, which is *transition*, its literal translation as well as what it really means to retire. I have a couple of close people in my life who say that they are retired. When I look at them, they are just as busy doing other jobs that are far from what people would consider retirement. Retirement, in my mind, should be total relaxation with the greatest of peace of mind. Retirement will be different for everyone. From day one at Depot, and up until my last few days, I was still going a hundred miles per hour. I would have to assume that there are a lot of people in this category. How do you go from hundred miles an hour to coasting on cruise control? You should be coasting if you are retired. This is another thing that we are never taught when we in the throes of our careers; it is called transition, the process of going from one state or condition to another. Change is often the catalyst of fear. Before I go too much further, I want to tell you what transition is *not*. If you retire one day from some position in your organization and then turn around and come back the next day working for the same organization, *that* is not a transition. I know that there may be some strong financial motivators to take this route, but from a transitions perspective, it may simply mean that you have put your retirement process on an indefinite hold.

The difficulty in this process will depend on how much you really enjoyed your job. I am really beating around the bush because, in the end, it is the strength of the emotional tie that you have to your career that will make the biggest difference. The stronger the tie, the harder the process will be. So those people that use the line from that old Johnny Paycheck cover "Take this Job and Shove It" should have no problem deciding to retire and move on to the next phase of their lives. For others, it may not be quite that easy. I consider this process similar to the stages of grief. Different people will transition through the various phases at much different speeds.

Who Am I?

For most, retirement is a conscious choice, meaning that it is within their control. There is no question that there will be some form of acceptance that you are no longer a police officer. You will not have the authority to arrest anyone, and this, in itself, may be a difficult adjustment for some. This is really what is behind the importance of knowing the answer the question "Who am I?"

In many ways, retirement from policing is similar to retirement from any other job, but it's the *difference* that will prove the most challenging. Dealing with the differences is like living on a different planet for over twenty years and then suddenly landing back on Earth to live out the rest of your life. It is somewhat similar to an astronaut returning to Earth after several months at the International Space Station. In his book, *An Astronaut's Guide to Life*, Chris Hadfield talks about his reintegration to Earth. He explains how living in a gravity-free environment has affected his speech and has caused his muscle mass and bone density to shrink. Something as simple as walking and talking posed a challenge for him when he got back to Earth. Luckily for Chris, he had a team of doctors to support him through these challenges.

During your reintegration to Earth from policing you may feel separation anxiety and isolation at the same time. You are no longer part of the police culture, a culture you placed your heart and soul in for so many years. It may even cause depression, but keep in mind that all these feelings are normal. Like Chris, you will have a team of professionals to lean on during your reintegration. You need to take the time to identify them in the event you need them.

I am very impressed with Veteran Affairs Canada. As soon as I submitted

You have to reconstruct your sense of self ...

my retirement papers, they were immediately engaged. In fact, I received a phone call at home, and during that conversation, they were looking to make a face-to-face appointment to determine if there were any physical or psychological ailments that I may have developed as a result of my career as a Mountie. This type of support, in addition to that of family and friends, will help you in your transition.

The notion of reconstruction as part of grieving is appropriate here. You have to reconstruct your sense of self, not necessarily building a *new* you, but rather expanding on the you that you are. You have just spent a number of years and had great successes, hardships, fun, and sorrow as a police officer, but this is only one chapter of your life. It may have been an extremely long one, but there should still be better chapters to come.

You can attend a pre-retirement seminar and google the web, but there is nothing that will truly prepare you for how you will react to your retirement. Since leaving the RCMP, I have run into retired members who are struggling with retirement. In one case, I didn't even have to ask how things were going; he was just being brutally honest. After the RCMP, he joined another police force and is now one of my colleagues. For him, the greatest challenge was being afraid of the unknown. He was lost the first time he retired, became bored and frustrated, and then ended up going back to work. That fear of the unknown can control us far more than we realize. Once in a while, you will see that look in a retiree's eyes – the look that says they miss being an active member and are struggling with something similar to separation anxiety. Then the question inevitably comes: "It's not the same, is it?" It is one of those questions that forces you to accept the fact that you are having difficulty dealing with the same sense of loss yourself but are afraid to admit it. I have to be honest that it has not been that easy for me. Funnily enough, I know that the best thing that I could ever do would be to listen to my own advice!

Deciding what to do with your time is a major part of transition.

Because of my personal situation, I eased myself out of my police officer practice into a less demanding career. If you still have the same motivation and drive to be just as successful in your second career, then all the power to you! Perhaps it would be wise to start looking at retirement as a practice as well. A few years ago, when I had well over twenty years' service, I decided to take a month off. I had never done this before, and I was looking forward to some relaxation. It did not take me too long to get bored. Much later on, my wife mentioned that, if I was going to do this again, to make sure that I have something to do because I was driving *her* crazy.

Deciding what to do with your time is a major part of transition. Some people may choose to get a part-time job or volunteer in the community, but I firmly believe that retirement should be about relaxing. If you are not used to relaxing, then you need to ease into it. No matter what you choose, your pace should slow while you assume control of what you do on a daily basis. Hopefully, the only schedule you will have to adhere to is the one that you set for yourself. Stop and think about all those times when you have been asked to engage in a social activity and your response has been, "No, I am sorry we cannot make it because I have to work." Now, what will your response be? You will have more options on how to spend your time as work is no longer the deciding factor. Once you are retired, your answer may become: "Let's make that happen. What date is good for you?"

Hopefully, retirement will turn out to be one adventure after another. It is like a second lease on life. Embrace this change as something that will spark great memories. I know that my wife has her plan in place and cannot wait to be a grandmother and be able to look after the little ones. Thanks to Ash and Riley she is on her way with Rowen.

We are here for a good time not a long time. When I was posted in Kelowna over ten years ago, I ran into Det. Al Catley, a Vancouver police detective who was working an unsolved homicide. He had a phrase he often used: "That's your life, mate." There are no second chances and we really need to live every day as if it is our last. When I was a kid, I dreamt about travelling to different places around the world so I could really experience what life is all about. Now that I am older and have a few miles on me, I look at it from a different perspective. I do want to travel, but I am more focused on what I want to do with my time. I want to do things with my family, like heading down to Mexico or visit Mickey and Minnie at Disney. If you decide to treat retirement as a practice, you would do it all and evaluate what gives you the greatest sense of accomplishment on an ongoing basis.

Chapter One Soundbites

- Always a means to an end
- An end is just a new beginning
- Make sure this end is always in the front

Chapter Two
THE FORCE — MAINTIENS LE DROIT

I'm dressed for success from my head down to my boots,
I don't do it for money ...
I don't do it for the glory, I just do it anyway.

"American Soldier"
—Toby Keith, 2003

Know History and Traditions

When I find myself lost in childhood memories, I begin to think about hot, humid summer days in Ottawa, our nation's capital. I think about how the grounds surrounding Parliament Hill were my playground, and eventually, I end up thinking about Canada Day. It is our nation's birthday, and on this day, there is mass chaos on the Hill. For one thing, the streets at the bottom of the Hill are lined with people waiting. My memory becomes vivid as the one thing they are all waiting for comes to life. I look up from where I stand nearby and I am in awe. Within my line of sight are those scarlet tunics, the full regalia of the RCMP on parade.

As I grew older, I learned more about the meaning behind this tunic. It not only echoes Canada's identity but reminds us all of a rich history that was born out of a nation's need for order in its own Wild Wild West. Its roots go back to the 1800s, when Sir John A. MacDonald, Canada's first prime minister, established the North-West Mounted Police to maintain law and order in the north-west portion of the Dominion of Canada. In 1904, it achieved a further distinction when it was given the *Royal* prefix by King Edward VII, going on to become the Royal Canadian Mounted Police in 1920.

If you were to look at any hat badge worn by a member of the RCMP, you would find the words "MAINTIENS LE DROIT", which means "Uphold the Right" or alternatively "Maintain the Right" and "Defend the Law." The unwritten part of this motto is the fact that members are expected to do this, even to the point of death. It is what Canadians have both enjoyed and come to expect with respect to the Force's international reputation: "The Mounties always get their man." Those Canadians who have altruistic values and a sense of pride in our nation may aspire to wear the red serge.

The RCMP developed a Mission, Vision, and Values statement long before it became popular across the federal public service. When it did become popular, it was an opportunity for the RCMP to encapsulate what they had already been doing since conception (See Appendix A).

Find Personal and Practice Meaning in "Maintiens le Droit"

Every member, every recruit, and every commissioned officer is duty bound to know and understand what this statement means and to apply it in their day-to-day work as a police officer. It sets the stage for any career in the Force. It is meant to set the tone and guide your conduct throughout your career and beyond. This is never etched in stone and is always subject to change. The change must always be seen in a positive light, motivated by the need to take the organization and its members to the next level. We should always sing from the same song book, but there is some flexibility because some can sing better in one key while others excel in another. Even those who sing out of key will find their own rhythm in keeping with the RCMP mission, vision, and values. In a sense, they were the Force's scripture, breathing life into what the Force needed to be as a whole. It is time the RCMP re-examined this and came to terms with what this means in a new generation of Mounties. This generation must find its own path and come to terms with what MAINTIENS LE DROIT means to them.

If you use these guiding principles, regardless of where your career takes you, you will likely have a positive self-image, feel a sense of accomplishment, and a belief that you have made a difference. Godspeed to you and enjoy your career as a peace officer! If you blink, you may miss it and all the joys, hardships, accolades and friendships that come with it.

Always dare to be great when you are young and know that, when you are no longer young, you can still always be great when you want to.

Attention! Forward, march!

Chapter Two Sound Bites
- Know your history and take time to celebrate it
- Know what the Big Picture is and what your corporate mantra is
- Find your own meaning for "Mission, Vision and Values"

Chapter Three
POLICING — A PRACTICE

Would you teach your children to tell the truth
Would you take the high road if you could choose...
Your Life is now

"Your Life is Now"
—John Mellencamp, 1998

Understanding the Jurisprudence and Applying It

The way we perceive ourselves has a powerful effect on how we act, where we belong and, most importantly, our level of self-confidence. When I was in high school, "life after high school" was always a topic under current affairs. Inevitably, the current affairs would move to medicine or law, both laden with prestige and characterized as having practices. A practice implies an expectation that one has never truly mastered the profession.

A few years ago, I realized how police work had evolved to the point where a higher standard of knowledge was needed just to get the job done. The police needed to be makeshift counselors, while knowing the law pertaining to the powers of arrest and gathering evidence, just as well as lawyers. The complexity of this need only continues to grow over time. It is a question of the balance between overriding an individual's rights for the protection of society with the expectation that police can do this with jurisprudence in mind.

As the courts render their decisions, there is the expectation that law enforcement completely understands the jurisprudence and its application. Meeting this expectation is not always that easy. It is one thing to understand it, but it is more challenging to apply it because no two situations are the same. What it does demonstrate is that, as a police officer, you are constantly learning and adjusting your trade craft, which supports the belief that law enforcement is also a practice.

Several dictionaries define a practice as a method, procedure, process, or rule used in a particular field or profession; a set of these regarded as standard. I began to look further at the definitions and found that it is also considered a business in which a professional or number of associated professionals offer services, such as a law practice or a medical practice.

These definitions can be easily applied to police work. There are a number of infrastructures in place that allow a police officer to develop their skill set in a number of disciplines or specialties. The specialties can range from being subject matter experts in drug investigations, serious crime investigations, commercial crime, statement taking, highway patrol, or even legal applications. The specialties are endless. Most aspire to plainclothes positions for the challenge and, in some cases, the status. The paths to the ultimate career destination will vary, but at the end of the day, the knowledge base will remain the same. In order to move towards any one specialty, all recruits, no matter which police force, all go through basic training of one sort or another.

Hitting the Streets

Like many new police officers, I hit the streets with the "pie in the sky" attitude of one poised to save the world. Coupled with the excitement was a sense of fear and apprehension. It did not take long to get over this and wake up to the reality of day-to-day police work. After a steady diet of street policing, I began to set my sights on other things, but I had no idea how to get from where I was to where I wanted to go. It was as if I was feeling my way around in the dark, just looking for the way. The one thing that I knew I could rely on and trust was my steady work ethic. Unfortunately, the work ethic would not be enough. Then it hit me, the key was a solid plan. Not unlike sound financial planning, I knew that I had to come up with something that would yield dividends later on in my career. I also knew that the plan had to be as flexible as possible, realizing that a career in policing would present a number of forks and bends in the road. In my case, the first fork in my road was deciding whether to go into drug work or serious crime.

Once you choose your path(s), you should strive to be the ultimate professional, which often requires self-reflection and introspection in order to transform yourself to meet both current and emerging needs. It is a cognitive rather than a physical transformation, and it requires a level of trust in yourself as the changes may be difficult to see at first. If police officers are expected to be constantly moving to a higher standard, then perhaps we should be accountable to one another as we move forward. Consider the following when making this change.

> **Walk into any given situation with the utmost confidence and with a specific end in mind.**

Always be "professionally aggressive" because, if you make this an expectation of yourself, it will not matter who you are dealing with, whether it be criminals in the street or one of many policing partners, such as Crown Counsel prosecutors. I define being professionally aggressive as walking into any given situation with the utmost confidence and with a specific end in mind. The specific end may mean getting what you want for yourself or your unit from upper management so they can perform their job better, or it may be as simple as coming to a compromise, but you need to know what your bottom line is before you walk into that situation. Always proceed in an ethical manner, leaving the door open for future positive contacts with these people. Building credibility and trust is one of the best things you can do, and it is *relatively* simple – you just need to keep your word. As you move to a higher level in the organization, you must have an in-depth knowledge of the subject matter in order to continue to build credibility. The ins and outs of being professionally aggressive will be influenced by your personality, and you will experiment at first, adopting your own style over time.

Master the Rules of Engagement

It also important to be a master of the rules, as policing has an abundance of laws and policies that are constantly changing. These form the rules of engagement for police work. If you become a master of these rules, you will, by extension, become more confident in your decisions. The fact that the rules are always changing means that you must constantly stay ahead of the curve. It is not difficult; you just have to be consistent. As an example, you should make a habit of reading case law as it relates to roadside stops in order to understand what you can and can't do when dealing with people on the streets. In the spirit of sharing learning, share your newfound knowledge with your colleagues. It will then be up to them to fully internalize the information and reflect on the significance it may have to their day-to-day jobs. As a master of these rules, you also need to know where the lines are and how far you can stretch them. This is important from a strategy development perspective, when trying to deal with an investigational issue or human resources issue. Sometimes knowing where the line lays means that you may end up hitting a wall. At that point, you may be forced to take a different route in order to meet the same end. The fact that you accomplished your goal and kept within the rules is a sign of being a true professional.

G.O.Y.A.A.T.T.P.

The police are in the people business.

Understanding how to be professionally aggressive in a law enforcement practice is not enough; one also has to understand how to be successful in this profession. The police are in the people business, which means that they need to know how to communicate with people at all levels of society and in all walks of life. For some people, this is easy, while others, have a hard time approaching people and having a meaningful business meeting, or trying to get a person to admit to a serious crime they've committed. In both cases, and regardless of your comfort level in doing this, you have to continually do it in order to become proficient, you must "G.O.Y.A.A.T.T.P."

There will be times when you meet people who will have a profound impact on your career. It is not unlike connecting with that favourite teacher in school. This is what happened to me when I was transferred to Yellowknife. On my first day, I met Rod, who was in charge of the detachment. He was a well-seasoned member and well versed in policing in the North. Rod carried himself with not only confidence, but also with a calm that just made you feel that everything was going to be all right, no matter what the crisis. When he spoke to you, it was always with you in mind and he had a personal message to deliver. When you listened to Rod, you would see this look in his eyes that clearly shouted excitement for policing.

Not long after that, he became the plainclothes commander. In this role, he was in charge of the detectives looking after the more serious matters. I then found myself on temporary assignment there, and one day he shared something with me. This was not "rocket appliances" (a *Trailer Park Boy's* expression), but it is the foundation of police work. It will never change, and the difference between a good policemen and a great policeman will be your ability to do this. It boils down to G.O.Y.A.A.T.T.P.

There is nothing better than a good war story, and Rod, hailing from Newfoundland, was always good for a few. One day, he broke into one of these stories about an investigation he had worked on. The crime happened in front of a house, and Rod was convinced that the woman who lived there must have witnessed this horrific event. He banged on her door, not once, not twice, but a number of times. Each time, the women denied seeing anything. He was relentless with his quest, and eventually, she confided that she had witnessed the crime and provided a crucial statement that would take the accused before the courts.

Why was Rod successful with this?

> **The challenge with today's society is that fewer and fewer people know how to engage in a real conversation.**

It was because of G.O.Y.A.A.T.T.P. (*get off your ass and talk to people*). Your ability to relate and to talk to anyone, no matter who they are, is crucial to your ability to solve crime and work with others, and it paves the way for future success. The challenge with today's society is that fewer and fewer people know how to engage in a real conversation. We are too busy sending emails, texting, or snapchatting, and we are slowly losing the ability to communicate face to face, often without realizing that an emoticon is just not doing the same job.

I have had the privilege of working with a lot of great people who understand the importance of talking to people. Sometimes though, talking is not enough, and you need to take it to the next level. This often means stepping outside of your comfort zone to do what needs to be done. When I think about moving beyond one's comfort zone, I immediately think about Ray. A few years ago, you would have found us in a small First Nations community, trying to pull the clues together to solve a historical murder. A lead then presented itself. We were led to believe that a witness existed and we were given the name of a woman. If this was actually the case, then we would be asking this individual to confide her deep, dark secret to perfect strangers.

The plan would be simple but the execution of the plan required some strategizing. How does one develop trust and some kind of bond with this woman so that she feels comfortable enough to share her level of involvement in a murder, all in a matter of minutes? In short, it meant pressing emotional buttons and knowing which button was the key to the information we needed. After careful deliberation, Ray and I were banging on her door with our strategy in hand. We identified ourselves as police officers and were invited in. Like any good door-to-door salesmen, we got to work with our own particular brand of sell job. After some time, it was evident that we were touching her emotions, but had not managed to find the right button. We intuitively knew that she was not ready to confide in us that day, and Ray wanted to keep the door open.

Thinking on the fly was the only strategy we had when Ray took action. While we were talking to her, there was a radio playing in the background. Ray walked over to this radio and looked at the woman. He began to dance to the Top 40 song, while looking directly at her. He told her that he wanted her to remember him and that if she was eventually willing to share any information with us, to simply remember him as the "dancing policeman." This is a good example of taking it to the next level. Police work is a people business, and you do what you need to in order to get people to confide in you. It is important to remember that the approach is ultimately dictated by your imagination and your comfort level. At that time, I am not sure if my comfort level would have allowed me to do what Ray did, but I do remember gaining a lot of respect for him. By now, you may be wondering how that particular homicide played out. As far as I know, it is still unsolved at the time of my writing this book. This was truly a swing and a miss, but it really set the stage for future successes for both Ray and myself. Today, Ray and I are great friends, but he never will forgive me for leaving him with that investigation when I transferred out of the North!

Effectively Guiding the Investigation

What is critical to remember is that there are no shortcuts in police work. The minute that you start taking shortcuts is the minute that you start making extra work for yourself in the longer term. It is slow, methodical work that requires an infinite amount of patience.

> **What is critical to remember is that there are no shortcuts in police work.**

This is clearly exemplified with respect to knowing how to guide an investigation based on the elements of an offence. Your investigation will mean nothing if you have not met the elements of the offence and you submit the report simply to get it off your plate. It will only end up coming back to you like a boomerang. This if far from being professional, and if you begin to adopt this behaviour, you will develop a less than stellar reputation with your colleagues, your supervisors, and outside partners. It can become a reflection of you and your organization. It can also get in the way of going where you want to go with your career.

You need support from others to move ahead in your career, and if they see you continually taking shortcuts or the easy way out, then your chances of success are between slim and none. I have seen this happen on a number of occasions. I have coined a term for this type of police work, and you want to avoid it like the plague. I call it "fast food policing." It is a term that speaks to police service delivery that is completed in a speedy fashion, but which may substantially lack in quality. It usually occurs in environments where there are high calls for service. The danger involved in this type of service delivery is it develops poor investigational habits. It leads to paper patrols, quick phone calls, and very little focus on actual service delivery. A *paper patrol* is a means of using creative writing to conclude a file and involves little or no investigation. Never forget, police work is a people business.

Technology in the People Business

In the last few years, technology has made it too easy to neglect our people business. Computers are designed to make our life easier, to get the job done quicker, allowing us to have more time to enjoy those things that life is really all about, such as playing golf, fishing, or making memories with our loved ones. Technology is a tool, and in police work, it is a tool in a people business. It is used to record data once we have that human interaction. It cannot become the tail wagging the dog. Keep in mind that you will likely meet the same people over and over again, and you want to develop positive relationships with them.

It had been a few years since I had been on the road, and when I returned, I certainly had my eyes opened. Change can be a great thing, but it is not *always* positive and it does not *necessarily* move you in the right direction. Information is now at an officer's fingertips. Patrol cars are equipped with computers so officers can go to calls, complete their resulting tasks, document their actions, and be available to take the next call without ever having to set foot in the detachment.

What seems to have been lost is the opportunity to develop relationships with your local contacts in the early morning hours when you see them out and about. These are commonly referred to as "street checks" and they are an excellent means of gathering intelligence as to what is going on in the streets. The scene would play out something like this. You would have a face-to-face visit in the wee hours of the morning. The usual banter would take place, including the obvious questions like "What are you doing out at this hour?" and "Where are you going?" This somewhat innocent conversation allowed you to make observations with respect to body language and what clothes the client was wearing, things that may or may not be important down the road. This information would be recorded in your notebook and you would share this in some format back at the office. This information could be instrumental in providing clues to a crime that happened in that same area of the check. What is even more important than the information you collected is the fact that you were building a relationship with these contacts.

Now, it is far too easy to drive up to these people without getting out of the vehicle, roll down the window, flip open the computer, tabulate any information worth noting, and then move on to the next person That is not enough if you are going to truly succeed as an investigator. You need to know your area inside out and that means establishing relationships with the people on the street. You must see this is an investment in your success as an investigator. I must admit that I was surprised when I heard that some officers were simply driving up to the person and having a chat, all the while typing everything into their computer. At first, I figured it was fast food policing but now it seems more like drive-thru policing.

Mistakes = Learning Opportunities

Expect that mistakes will be made along the way. These are opportunities to develop yourself as a professional. There are very few of us who have a natural ability to do everything at a master's level. Some learning curves are steeper than others, depending on the task at hand. The harder the task, the greater the likelihood you will make an error, or looking at it from the flip side, actually creates an opportunity. Errors or missteps, if properly recognized and navigated, can actually lead to later successes.

Errors or missteps, if properly recognized and navigated, can actually lead to later successes.

You will have to learn to trust your supervisors with helping you learn from mistakes. They will expect the mistakes, and it is their job to work with you to ensure that the same mistake does not happen again in the future. I believe there is nothing that speaks more directly to our professional integrity than how we deal with our mistakes. In the Force, it is often referred to as "falling on the sword" but it is more than that. It is not enough to fall on your sword; you also have to take some concrete action to show that you understand what you have done wrong and what you are going to do to ensure it doesn't happen again.

I remember the first lecture I gave on a national course. It was a national disaster. The topic was too important, and I dropped the ball. I felt sick to my stomach over it, and knew I had to fix it. I promised myself that this would not happen again, as there was too much at stake. I attacked it from two fronts. The first was going beyond general knowledge of the subject matter and knowing it upside down and backwards. The second and, the more challenging for most, was to stand up in front of my peers and effectively communicate with the hopes of increasing understanding of a difficult subject. This is where John stepped in and took me under his wing. John was my partner when I was a sergeant on the Legal Applications Support Team, and also a university professor. He would give me pointers, watch me lecture, and give me more pointers. To this day, if he is watching one of my lectures, I look forward to his feedback.

When you make a mistake, you have a responsibility to "make it good." This was a life lesson that hit me right between the eyes years ago, while working a homicide investigation. I was one of three investigators, and we used every investigative technique you could think of, including an undercover operation. The undercover technique relies on a number of scenarios that are goal oriented. An operator will meet with the suspect in order to meet the goal of the day. This is extremely challenging for an undercover operator, and mistakes *will* happen. Each undercover operation has an assigned coverman. Like a director in a movie, the coverman will create the scenarios and direct the operator as to the goal in each scenario. There is incredible pressure on the undercover officer, for any misstep or failure to follow direction could cause your investigation to go down the toilet. I am not really sure what the goal was in this particular scenario, but the operator fell short and even to the point of compromising the operation. During the debriefing, the coverman simply said three words: "Make it good." This was said with confidence and there was no question regarding what the operator had to do. In the next scenario, the undercover operator made it good. This is a short story but a valuable one in understanding how to overcome mistakes. It is how we deal with our mistakes that will make a difference. In the words of Billy Joel: "We're only human, we're supposed to make mistakes." The challenge in police work is that the stakes are always so high and the belief is that we cannot afford to make mistakes.

Evolving Your Police Practice

When you begin as a police officer, you tend to be a jack of all trades and master of none. It is a little like being a kid in a candy shop, looking around and trying to decide which discipline to develop your practice in. In a literal sense, practice means doing something over and over again until you reach some level of proficiency, and by *some level* I mean that there will always be a higher level you should aspire to, regardless of the discipline. Your discipline should be something you enjoy doing, a job that gets you excited to get out of bed every morning and go to your practice. In my case, I started with taking statements and, in particular, getting our clients to admit to their involvement in crime. Early in my service, I was constantly bringing people back to the detachment and talking to them in the interview room.

That changed halfway through my practice when I had an opportunity to write wiretap warrants. I did this for two years straight, and it allowed me to get to a comfortable level of proficiency, and I would later get to another level when I worked with our Legal Application Support Team. This team has a fantastic reputation for helping investigative teams advance their investigations. This was initially in the form of giving advice on wiretap investigations, but it also included sound advice specific to investigational strategy. It was always exciting work as we got to touch the most high-profile cases in the province and, sometimes, even the country. Being in that role meant that you always had to keep current. And *that* meant keeping up with case law, attending seminars, and keeping relationships intact with other experts to keep abreast of the changes.

Remember, a practice really means to practice a skill set or activity over and over again.

This is a clear demonstration of the expectation of having a practice in law enforcement. Make it your expectation.

What is important for your practice is that you not only create learning plans, but that you be committed to their execution. These plans must be practical and facilitate the achievement of a level of proficiency in your practice. Remember, a practice really means to practice a skill set or activity over and over again. During your practice in law enforcement, you must take advantage of the courses, workshops, and seminars that are available to you. They should be included in your learning plan. That being said, you cannot wait for the course to come along before you start practicing. The training that law enforcement officers are offered today is fantastic, and in theory, we are turning out better police officers. What is crucial though is the application of the knowledge that is gained through that training. So many times, I have heard people say. "I can't do this or I can't do that because I have not had the course." You do not need to have the course to begin to practice at a lower proficiency level.

I remember having a conversation with one of our Training NCOs on this topic. He mentioned a member who was well known for his ability to interview and interrogate. Interviewing and interrogation requires a lot of practice to become effective at any level of proficiency. The Training NCO told me that this officer had never taken the course. How could this be? A person highly respected for this ability had never been formally trained. I laughed and told him that I had never taken our Warrant Writing course or Affidavit Writing course either, and I was considered a subject matter expert.

Make a Commitment to Your Practice

You have to take the initiative and make the commitment to your professional development. Your career will go by far too quickly, with no time for second chances, so be sure you're able to look back and have no regrets. Afford yourself every opportunity to learn as you want to get the most out of your practice and really be the best that you can be. If you adopt this approach, and then you finally get that course you've been waiting for, it may simply reaffirm that what you have been doing in your practice is appropriate. I think that is one of the reasons that, when you are completing a course critique and it comes to the part that addresses the appropriateness of the training at this point in your career, you should always want to say you wished you could have had it sooner. More often, it will just give you more confidence in your abilities and motivate you to strive for the next level of proficiency.

Professional Ethics – Do the Right Thing at the Right Time

No matter what, professional ethics should always be in the forefront. To keep it as practical and simple as possible, the integrity of policing really boils down to doing the right thing at the right time. As with most things, this is easier said than done. I am not convinced that you can really *teach* ethics. You can, however, teach individuals what the expectations are when it comes to ethical behaviour.

> **Teach individuals what the expectations are when it comes to ethical behaviour.**

When trying to choose ethical leaders, I think the challenge arises because it is sometimes difficult to adequately assess ethical behaviour. When I was competing for a promotion, I was required to provide examples of situations where I was confronted with an incident that required me to do the right thing. The problem with this approach is that it is self-serving. Some professional organizations rely on peer assessments to verify the demonstration of such behaviours. This seems to take things one step further, but it assumes that those peers are going to honestly assess the individual.

Ethical behaviour consists of two parts:
1. Understanding what the right thing to do is
2. Having "courage of conviction"

In my mind, courage of conviction is really the key, and it is the true reflection of ethical behaviour. What this means is not necessarily different from person to person. It means doing the right thing, even when people disagree or oppose you. I will propose a twist to this, and you can evaluate it based on your own experience and/or perceptions.

So you come to the conclusion what the right thing to do is but you become afraid that it will make you look bad and affect your career. You see historically no one has really dealt with the issue even though it has serious consequences. You minimize the consequences and convince yourself to overlook it. In this case the whole organization knows what the right thing to do is but it has been overlooked. If you get yourself into a habit of asking "What is the right thing to do?" each and *every* time, and then act then your courage of conviction comes with ease. It is really a matter of being selfless.

It is not always easy, and this is why there is whistleblower policy that encourages this type of positive behaviour. This is a very important standard for any type of practice, and it is at the heart of its integrity. What is even more important to remember is that, as law enforcement professionals, the ethical standard for our practice will always be higher in the eyes of the public and government. This can become a little blurry as you rise through the ranks. It is a constant challenge knowing that, by doing the right thing in one situation; it can cause a ripple effect that ends up being the wrong thing for another situation. This means that you will have more *masters* to consider, weigh, and mitigate in determining the right action for both the good of the organization and of the public.

The police universe needs to take a different perspective on this and begin by accepting it is a practice. It really means that someone must champion this cause with a mind to continually developing best practices and, more importantly, the best people in police work. It means setting a higher standard for law enforcement that will translate to a higher standard in the context of service delivery. This begins by accepting the fact that police work is fluid, which depends on the political climate and/or the presence of crime. It means being flexible to ensure growth and higher levels of proficiency.

Chapter Three Sound Bites
- Be professionally aggressive and the ultimate professional
- Policing is a practice; approach it that way
- The art of communication needs appreciation
- Be uncomfortable to be comfortable

Chapter Four
LOOKING OUT FOR NUMBER ONE

You'll find out the only way to the top is lookin' out for number one,
I mean you, keep looking out for number one

"Looking Out for Number One"
—Randy Bachman, 1981

The alarm clock goes off. It is 4:00 a.m. You wake up, shower while you are still half asleep, and make it to the office by 6:00 a.m. You walk through the door at the office, greet your team, and head to your desk. You get the 411 (information) on the previous shift, but you also pay close attention to any officer safety concerns, along with information relating to investigations under your conduct. You make some phone calls, set up some interviews, and hit the streets. Your shift is almost over, and you need to get back to the office to attempt some paperwork and, before you know it, it is 5:00 p.m. Now, it is time to head home to your family.

The alarm clock goes off. It is 4:00 am. You wake up, shower while you are still half asleep, and make it to the office by 6:00 a.m. You walk through the door at the office, greet your team, and head to your desk. Suddenly, you realize that your life has become an updated version of *Ground Hog Day*.

In this movie, Bill Murray starred as a weatherman re-living the same day over and over until he understands what is important in his life, causing the time loop to be broken. He finally got it right! What "getting it right" means is not the same for everyone. Before I left the RCMP, I often joked that I would be back the next day until I got it right. For me, getting it right meant that I could move on to the next stage, retirement.

Police work is routine and monotonous, with only a hint of excitement. It is similar to watching major league baseball. There is a sense of anticipation in the air, and the fans are looking for that go ahead run tie the ballgame. The batter comes to the plate, the pitcher eyes the runner on third base, and throws the ball. A swing and a miss, strike one! Not long after, it is full count and the anticipation of the crowd has turned to tension. The ball is thrown, the batter knocks in the go ahead run and the crowd roars. The play is over in a matter of seconds, and the crowd quiets down for the next batter. In police work, it is always a World Series game, and your go ahead run is your next investigation.

Establish Your Best Practice Habits Early

If the Crown Counsel report is done poorly, all your hard work is for nothing.

You will work on an investigation for hours, days, months, or sometimes *years* before an arrest is made. The stars become aligned when an opportunity presents itself for your magical play, and you make the arrest. The reason for all of the routine stuff of collecting evidence, conducting interviews, and mundane paperwork makes sense now that success is within your reach.

It is like finding the Cadbury secret for success, but you quickly learn that, if you do not stick to the secret recipe, your success is varied. A big part of that formula will be the mundane paperwork that inevitably ends with a Crown Counsel report. This report is the basis for the decision to prosecute and needs to be done right or there will be no conviction. If the Crown Counsel report is done poorly, all your hard work is for nothing, the high fives back at the office just went down the drain. The people you arrested are back on the streets, have a notch under their belt for beating the charge, and are primed for their next crime. It is worse than that though, for you have let down the victims who were violated and traumatized. Your reputation as a TNI (top notch investigator) is suspect, and you have chipped away the public confidence in the police. It is, in short, a fail.

Without well-established habits, the pattern of failure continues. Ideally, you want to start your habits early in your career so that you are on the right path, but it is never too late. It took me some time to realize the importance of habits. It also impressed upon me the importance of having a great trainer, one who will put the screws to you when you're falling behind. Field trainers are selected for various reasons and have an incredible influence on how the tone is set for a young officer's career. In my case, my trainer had the gift of the gab and could develop intelligence for any crime that happened in town. What was missing was the proper clean-up or paperwork.

I established my own habits and focused on those routine, mundane tasks. I was on the road to becoming a better cop, but it was still a challenge. I would still find myself with overdue assignments, and after several calls to my boss's office, I knew I had to fix this and quickly.

With a little introspection about my work habits, I found the answer: I could take a time management course and my problems would be solved. The RCMP offered short correspondence courses, and I immediately ordered the course materials. The truth is, I never finished the course. I could not find the time. I tried again a few years later, but again, I could not seem to find the time.

Your success is dependent on you finding the time. Remember, you are a professional, and you are developing a practice in police work without relying on shortcuts. Believe me, at one point, you will see the payoff for all of your efforts. I did eventually find the time, but it was in my way. I started to develop my own habits, and eventually they became second nature. This created momentum, resulting in more arrests, convictions, and public confidence, not to mention becoming a stronger contender for promotion.

One of the habits I did take from my short exposure to my failed time management courses was the use of a *to do list*. This is essentially a personal management tool that has to be used properly if it is to be effective. I do not know how many times I returned from leave and was behind the eight-ball when I started my list. In no time at all, I had listed fifteen tasks, then twenty. I felt like I had never taken leave and my anxiety level was rising. There was no way I could address all the tasks on the list and still take new calls.

Priority Management

To use the list effectively, it needs to be practical, and *you* need to be flexible. The list is a living document, with changing priorities. In order to make this habit work, the list should have no more than five items. Out of these five, you will have things that must be done immediately, while the others will be of a less urgent nature. Always include a task that contributes to your development in this top five. This task should be aligned with your career path. For example, if you are interested in drug work, you may put a drug investigator's course on your list and figure out how to get that training or find a way to schedule a meeting with the person in charge of your drug unit so that you can get some sage advice on how to get from A to Z.

If you are so inclined, you may include team building or networking events. These are great for relationship building. There should also be a balance between work and family functions.

The *To Do List*

Making your list should be as automatic as breathing, make it the first task of your day. My lists were always in my notebook, and that allowed me to go back and look at my previous lists to see that one item that continued to appear. This gave me an indication of where I needed to focus my efforts because I knew I needed to complete this task first. I set up my notebook so that the top page was dedicated to what I needed to speak about at my watch briefs and then, directly under that, was my list. My list would include categories such as emails, phone calls, meetings, development actions and projects that I had on the side of my desk. As an alternative, you can make your list near the end of your shift as long as you are consistent with one or the other.

In a perfect world, you would make your list and the complete your task, but the problem with policing is that it has a habit of interrupting the best laid plans. Expect this, as it will happen time and time again. If you are consistent with this process, you will still get more work done, even amid interruptions. Think of it like financial planning, where each completed task is an investment in your future and, over time, you will benefit from the compounded interest in knowledge and experience. Even in those locations that are less prone to interruptions, it is still a habit that should be developed early in your policing career.

To guarantee your success, develop your practice like a general contractor. This sounds like multi-tasking, but it is far from it. At one point, success was built on an individual's ability to multitask, but trends today suggest that, when there are several tasks on the go simultaneously, the work does not always get completed and the tasks that *do* get done are not necessarily completed to the highest standard of performance. The reality of police work is that there is a multitask element to the work, and how you manage juggling those tasks will have a direct impact on your success. The *to do list* is a tool that assists with this juggling. It is more a question of how you are going to keep track of all your tasks you have on the go.

A general contractor normally has several building projects on the go, some are just at the foundation level while others are at the landscaping stage. In the context of police work, in some investigations, you are just receiving the complaint, whereas others have you in court giving evidence. As a general contractor, you need to have a good sense of the stage of each investigation as this will help focus priorities. In business, one way of tackling it is by using a Gantt chart, which allows you to manage multiple components of a project at the same time. The chart will contain start and finish date as well as the progress made on a particular aspect of the project. This is the monitoring element of the chart. It helps to ensure that you keep an eye on the big picture.

Be selfish, but in a smart way. You can complete all your assignments quickly, with high level of quality, and hurry home, but you may be ultimately letting yourself down. It is like working for twenty-five years and not having a pension plan. You walk out the door and get the "Thanks for coming" speech and what do you actually have to show for those twenty-five years? It is your career and you must be professionally aggressive with it. Your learning plan should always contain some components that can be placed on your *to do list*. That learning element should be part of your top five.

It may be something as simple as completing an online course that is a prerequisite for a classroom course. It may be developing a relationship either inside or outside of your police force. In this case, the purpose of the relationship is to assist with your development, so you are looking for a person who will give you sage advice or perhaps help develop you in a certain skill set. As an example, in the fine art of interrogation, I would get to know the subject matter experts on a first name basis. As a start, just reach out to your resident experts and develop those relationships as you begin to hone your craft in whatever direction you pursue. Discipline yourself with the items on your list because these items will pay you the most return. In order to address each item in a timely manner, create a sense of urgency and set a deadline; you are in the driver's seat, so you can decide when you want to have a course completed by or when you will reach out to someone for help in your development. This process should become a habit, no different than the actual *to do list*.

Doing just that *little* bit more can make the ultimate difference in your career. It does not matter if you have been on the job one day or a thousand days; this process will help to put things in perspective. The secret is not to kill yourself, but just do a little bit more than everyone else. If you do just ten percent more over time, it will position you well to obtain that transfer or promotion to a position you've set your sights on. I say "position you well" because there are factors that are out of your control when such decisions are being made. Just have confidence and be satisfied with your efforts because they will get you to where you want to go. It may not be when you want it, or it may be in a totally different direction than you anticipated, but these are often blessings in disguise.

The last position I held was far from what I was shooting for, but ended up being very fulfilling for me. I remember the discussion I had with our human resources officer, and I was not sure whether I was being stroked, but I was flattered. He likened my abilities as a police officer to the Great Gretzky as a hockey player. When it comes to transfers, it is never *only* about you; the needs of the organization always have to come into play as well. I think, when we end up somewhere completely different than expected, that destiny has played a part, and there should be acceptance and *possibly* even gratitude. This does not necessarily mean that "you don't always get what you want, but you get what you need." It matters not; it is still an opportunity and a new starting point.

Work Smart and Teach Others

It was time for me again, even at my rank, to take a look around and see what the ten percent factor was. It is all about being consistent, time after time. The ten percent factor is really about having a good sense of your work environment from an output perspective. You are looking at what everyone is doing and

Share what you learn with your peers so that you continually foster the teamwork environment ...

what kind of effort they are putting in, and *your* plan will be to just do a little bit more than that. This can be in the context of personal development, or volunteering for those projects that will present themselves. It will be the consistent ten percent that will make the difference over the long run. Your career is going to be a long haul, so you want to run a marathon and not a sprint. The ten percent will have so many benefits. Your supervisors will begin to notice the extra effort and begin to reward you with a little extra work. Whether it is a reward or not, will depend on how you manage it; you do not want to burn yourself out. It is a sign that your work is paying off, and it presents an opportunity to develop yourself to a higher level. Whatever the opportunity, do not forget to share what you learn with your peers so that you continually foster the teamwork environment approach to work.

If your aspirations are to climb the ranks quickly, then do more than ten percent. You will have to be careful with this as well. Climbing high, too quickly, can be dangerous as well. Aside from burnout, you may have a challenge with your credibility because you have not learned what you needed in the trenches, the experience that demonstrates to people that you have also "walked the talk."

Know Yourself and Your Limits

From a financial perspective, ten percent could be a rule of thumb, but I must to caution you here. There is lots of money to be made in overtime hours. It can come to you automatically, or you can go looking for it. When I was working homicide, the overtime was a blessing in disguise. I was at a time in my life when I was moving away from a relationship and had incurred some debt that I needed to get rid of fast. The problem with overtime is that it is like heroin. You have this extra chunk of cash every month, and you begin to spend it and start liking the lifestyle this extra cash is allowing you to enjoy. It feels good to live like this, and it almost justifies the time you are taking way from your family when you are working the extra hours. Like heroin, you start with a little and, before you know it, you are hooked and crave more. To support your habit, you work more overtime, and the cycle repeats itself. Then the worst thing happens, the tap is turned off.

Once you are transferred to a location with little or no overtime, the reality sets in. In order to compensate, you have to go looking for more. The next thing you know, you are working at other units on your days off, just to keep your habit going. This will burn you out, and you will eventually crash. If you want to work overtime, and you have a financial goal in mind, then it is a great opportunity. Just know yourself and your limits. I worked in a unit where I could work endless hours of overtime, but I chose not to because I knew the gravy train was going to end, and I was easing the blow for my next move. As a watch commander, I did not work any overtime. The twelve-hour shifts can be great if you work them properly and get the most you can out of your time. This will then allow you to enjoy your time off to recharge your batteries. Just know what your limits are, and listen to both your body and the people around you; they will let you know that you need to slow down before you reach the burnout stage.

Get to Know Policy

Stimulate your mind by reading something work-related every day. Take fifteen minutes and either read policy or law (statute or case). The understanding of policy and law is essential if you want to do your job well. In the paper world, each detachment had operational and administration manuals and you were expected to read them. Read material that is topical to your duties. Policy is really the how-to guide. It is always the "go to" with any investigation, as it helps to get you from A to B. With the evolution (or devolution) of computers, you have to search these manuals electronically. This was not always an easy task, given the quality of the search engine, but regardless, the message is the same – get to know policy. Start with operational, and then move to administrative policy. They are both equally important. Understanding law is vital. Reading it develops your confidence in using your authorities. If you want to review your powers of arrest, search, or elements of an offence, you will find it here. If you get in the habit of reading case law, you will be miles ahead of your colleagues. It is setting up your edge. You need to become an expert at doing this; it is part of your practice.

Each and every day, keep your eyes and ears open and treat it as an opportunity to learn from someone, no matter who they are or what they are doing. Everyone has a story and a wealth of life experiences that a lot of us miss along the way. At my first post, there was this guard named Marv. He was a crusty old retired Windsor police officer, but there was still a lot of fight left in him. It must have been great for Marv to relive his glory days, watching us grow up as policemen right in front of him. It was a hot, busy summer day in northern Alberta, and I was being run ragged. I had just finished booking another drunk, and there was a lull. Marv must have seen this as his opportunity, so he began to speak. It was if, all of a sudden, I was that drifter, riding that railcar in the Kenny Roger's song, "The Gambler." He looked at me and told me that, at times, police work would make you feel like you were being beat up, but to keep doing it because, in the end, it will pay off. These small words of encouragement meant the world to me and impressed on me the need to always stretch myself.

Finding the limit is a challenge, but in all honesty, we should have no limits. To me, with setting a limit comes the word *can't*, and this word does not exist in my vocabulary. "Do or do not. There is no try." Who knew that George Lucas's little green alien would have such an impact on our lives? Push

> "Do or do not. There is no try." —Yoda

yourself, but in a healthy way. Trust the people you are working with to pull you aside and let you know if you are stretching yourself too thin. It was great having people telling me they had too much on their plates. This was great from a couple of perspectives. It meant that I had created an environment for them to trust me and be comfortable in sharing this important information, but it also meant that I had to manage the team a little differently to allow someone to get caught up, whether emotionally, physically or task-wise.

When I hear people say that they are too busy, I believe that they are putting a limit on themselves. It is the old monkey story, where researchers place a few monkeys in a cage along with a bunch of bananas. When the monkeys approach the bananas, they are doused with water – and they move away from the bananas. This continues until the monkeys become conditioned and will not go anywhere near the bananas. New monkeys are introduced with the old. The new monkeys move towards the bananas and are held back by the old monkeys. The new monkeys are initially confused, but they begin to follow suit with the old monkeys. The same thing can happen when you look at being "too busy". What if the new people did not know they were busy, and simply followed what I have been suggesting? Being busy all of the time is not healthy, but thinking that you are busy when you are *not* is worse and causes just as much damage from a stress perspective.

When you are out in your PC (police cruiser), make a habit of jumping on the next call. I worked on a watch (police shift), up North that had a great team environment, with everyone watching out for everyone. There were lots of calls for service up there, but we survived it by working as a team. If you take this tack, even the busiest and most stressful of times at work can become a bit of a game, making for some healthy competition. There were times when our team could not keep up with the calls for service. Our inherent sense of teamwork helped us to get the job done and let us have fun with one another.

Find Your Centre Each Day

Make sure you take a sanity break every day. No matter how bad your day is at work, it is never as bad as the people you are dealing with on the streets. You will see people at their worst and you need to come up with an effective way of coping. Take a moment and smell those roses. When I was in Kelowna – especially during the night shift – I would find myself on the crest of this hill. When you hit the crest, it was like you could see forever. The view was spectacular. You could see the lake and the rolling hills, and at night, all the lights made it just that much more magical. For a brief time, and I mean a *brief* time, I was in awe, and I found a sense of peace and comfort from this particular view.

The same thing happens to me when I ride the ski lift to the top of Big White and take the time to stop and look around instead of heading down right away. I remember doing this at Whistler a few years back. It was a gorgeous, sunny day, and I was alone on this hill; the mountain was mine. What a great feeling. It does not take long to do something like this, and what you accomplish is not only a mental break, it also takes you back to centre. In your case, it could be a pond, a mountain, or it could simply be stopping by a sports field to watch soccer or football. You can even take it one step further. It has done wonders for me coaching with the Chilliwack Giants Minor Football Association. Finding and appreciating these breaks is really one of the most important rituals you can develop.

Chapter Four Sound Bites
- Look out for #1, but take as many people as you can along the way
- Develop your own recipe for success, knowing ingredients change over time
- A little is really is a lot

Chapter Five
LIFE/WORK BALANCE

And as I hung up the phone, it occurred to me,
He'd grown up just like me.
My boy was just like me.

"Cats in the Cradle"
—Harry Chapin, 1973

Stress Awareness Means Survival

Life/work Balance (LWB). What does it mean? Is it something you can capture in some container and simply spoon out a few helpings when you need it? Is it something so fluid that it's like trying to nail Jell-O to the wall? It will be different for everyone because we all lead different lives.

LWB is everyone's elephant that needs to be talked about over and over again. Police work causes unrealistic and unknowing stresses to both you and your family. You must take care of yourself to be of value, both at home and at work, with the ultimate goal surviving so that you can enjoy retirement. At one point, I was dealing with a psychologist who was helping the members and staff cope with a traumatic incident. I met with him to give him the background of the incident causing the trauma. In this short meeting, he told me that if he could ensure that a retiring member was not an alcoholic or suffering from depression, he would meet his goal. He believed that we pay enough doing our day-to-day job and that we should not continue to sacrifice ourselves after the job is done.

This is something that I have struggled with throughout my career. It is a struggle because your environment is always changing, and you need to learn to listen to yourself, your friends, and family, in order to know when you are stressed. For half my service, I worked in serious crime. These investigations are front-end loaded. This means that the investigation is heavily resourced within the first week or more because that is the best time to gather evidence of the crime. It involves around the clock shifts with little sleep in between.

This is stressful on you, both physically and mentally, not to mention your family, who are alone while you are engaged in these investigations. As a watch commander, I provided frontline service in a place with a high volume of work, and in cases involving a significant amount of violence, where drugs and alcohol were a factor. My watch always struggled to finish one complaint before the next one came in. It is a fast-paced, high stress environment, and you need to maintain your health. I was always mindful of this and reminded my team of the importance of taking leave and thinking about LWB.

At twenty-seven years of service, I began to appreciate what LWB meant. It was always on my mind during my service, but I had difficulty with my follow through. A few years ago, I decided to get a tattoo. Tattoos are, or *should* be, personal and have some sort of meaning. You are literally branding yourself for life. I thought long and hard in my personal search for the perfect symbol that would reflect a piece of what I was feeling, who I am, or in this case, what I should always remember. I had an epiphany: I wanted a symbol that meant balance. It would be a poignant reminder of what I should always have and cherish. In my mind, no symbol says balance better than the Yin Yang, and I set out to research it. Now think about this, Yin Yang is a symbol that subscribes to the belief that opposite or contrary forces are actually complementary. A pragmatic look at the symbol might just indicate two opposing forces trying to find balance. This was merely a reflection of how important it is to have LWB and a reminder to pay attention and always take action to get back to that centre point.

Shortly after getting the tattoo, I was in Kelowna for a homicide trial. I was with my old partner, Lisa, and another colleague, and I decided to take a swim. My tattoo was exposed and the question came out "Why the Yin Yang?" Before

I could say anything, Lisa spit out the word "balance". I am not sure whether she related to the symbol herself or just knew me well enough, but I am sure that the Yin Yang was the right brand for me.

Manage Personal Stress Daily

Let's be honest with ourselves, stress can kill you. It shows no mercy, and it sneaks up on you. I attended a retirement party for a friend whom I had not worked with in years. As a young recruit, I looked up to this person and

> Stress can kill you. It shows no mercy and it sneaks up on you.

his successes. I wanted to be just like him. As I sat at the party, I learned that, about a year prior, he had had a heart attack and this strongly influenced his decision to retire. He had given his life and soul to the Force; I can only imagine that, if he had placed LWB as a consideration on day one of his career, he would have been leaving the Force under different circumstances.

Police work presents so many different types of stressors that learning how to manage them should be a daily practice. This means that you have to develop your own personal strategies for dealing with stress. This can encompass a wide range of activities: exercise, reading, family dinners, meditation, or getting away from it all. The good thing about family vacations is that they are most often planned in advance. Make them a ritual and you will begin to develop unforgettable memories that will last a lifetime. The same can be said for family dinners, try and have them at least once a month. Perhaps, instead of dinner, a round of golf will work for you, yoga or a walk on your favourite trail. These are not chores; these are opportunities to re-charge, together with your friends and family.

In the past, it was not uncommon to lean on the bottle as an acceptable means of dealing with work stressors, but this has caused far more damage than it's worth to people over the years. But how do you develop your personal strategy to cope with stress over the years? Keep in mind that it needs be personal because we all react to things differently based on our upbringings and life experiences, but the physical and psychological manifestations are the same from individual to individual. It is a matter of first understanding that there are real and recurring stressors in police work.

Your coping mechanism depends on the type of stressor and its severity. Secondly, and more importantly, you need develop a sense of self-awareness so that you can effectively manage the effects of the stressors. At times, the stress can be handled by simply taking time off or by talking with your loved ones. At other times, it may involve taking advantage of professional help. Having a strategy is essential to dealing with those times when you feel that there is a perfect storm brewing – times when the job has knocked the wind out of you and you're also dealing with significant family issues.

There is a part of the job that all the training in the world can never prepare you for. It involves a number of firsts: your first sudden death, your first fatal motor vehicle accident, and your first homicide. These scenes are not a part of normal, everyday life. It is not normal to see these scenes, and they never truly leave you; even one of these is traumatic enough to scar you for life. You need to accept that they will affect you and be prepared to deal with them time and time again. When I start to think about my firsts, the pictures are always vivid in my mind.

When I was in Yellowknife, we were called to investigate a sudden death. There had been an explosion in one of the mines that resulted in a death. Scenes like these are always treated as if a crime has occurred unless we know otherwise. I was given the unenviable task of being the exhibit officer, which meant seizing hundreds of items that were pieces of the puzzle to assist in explaining what had happened. For a week, we went deep underground in the mine to process the scene. It was what that explosion did to the victim that made it far more challenging to see and deal with. It was like a scene from *Saving Private Ryan*.

A member of our investigative team came to me and had the courage to confide that this scene really bothered him. In this officer's case, he had previously worked at a detachment that was on a major highway where he attended countless fatal motor vehicle accidents. The mine accident was the proverbial straw that broke the camel's back, and it gave him a wakeup call. It was the cumulative effect of witnessing all these horrific events over the years, until his body and mind finally told him that they had had enough.

As a police officer, you get pretty adept at compartmentalizing these types of events, but you can never ignore them. The moment that you ignore them, they will come back to bite you. This is when you will be knocked flat on your face. This officer was smart enough to know that he did not like the way he was reacting, and he dealt with what he was experiencing rather than ignore it.

Debrief Support Staff Who Were Involved

In today's workplace, we are wise enough to have psychological debriefings to help officers manage this type of stress. We are doing a better job of this than in the past, but we are far from perfect. The debriefing has to be done right away, or it has no value; to do it after the fact is merely an exercise in checking the boxes. The whole point of the debriefing is to deal with the feelings and emotions that arise as a result of being a witness to horrific events. If it is not conducted right away, those feelings and emotions blow around in the wind, only to pop up elsewhere, often in an unhealthy way. These briefings should not be restricted to investigative team members only. Any support staff member who has provided assistance, should also be included. Chances are these individuals have seen the photos of the scene or read the reports, and they will have been affected as well.

The realization that you are experiencing a high level of stress may come to you from someone else who is a friend, co-worker, spouse, or from anyone for that matter. This may be in the form of a

Always keep in mind that emotion knows no reason.

harmless comment out of concern, pointing out that you have been either edgy lately or simply not yourself. Your first response to this will likely be denial – or possibly even aggression. If you ever find yourself in that situation, consider the 24-hour rule. Always keep in mind that emotion knows no reason. Your initial response is based purely on emotion, but if you are starting to wear down psychologically, then reason will be your strongest ally. I would suggest stepping back, attempting some introspection to examine the comments that have been made. Chances are, you will find some truth in what has been said by someone who was courageous enough to bring it to your attention. This is a great step forward in self-awareness, but there must also be some follow through. Everyone needs a support system, and your significant other will hopefully be at the top of the list. It can include a best friend or a religious advisor if you are so inclined. You should also be aware that this support system might not be the solution that you are looking for in every situation, and that, in some instances, you should seriously consider professional help.

Post-Traumatic Stress Disorder

Back in the "good old days," we were supposed to be tough as nails, and to believe that all the graphic violence was part of the job, and that you simply had to accept it. If you were having difficulty in dealing with these horrific events and/or images, it was seen as weakness. Members were afraid that this weakness would result in a stigma being attached to them. The tough-as-nails philosophy evolved with the best of intentions, but it has caused significant damage over the years and has likely resulted in more stress. More recently, I have heard the term post-traumatic stress disorder (PTSD) bantered around quite a bit, and more than anything, I was curious about it. I had heard the term, time and time again, as it related to soldiers coming back from the war, but I had no idea what it meant or how it occurred within police work and with other first responders, such as paramedics and firefighters. I looked into it further to raise my own awareness.

PTSD is defined as a mental illness. It involves exposure to trauma, involving death or the threat of death, serious injury, or sexual violence. PTSD causes intrusive symptoms, such as re-experiencing the traumatic event. Many people have vivid nightmares, flashbacks, or thoughts of the event that seem to come from nowhere. They often avoid things that remind them of the event, for instance, someone who was hurt in a car crash may avoid driving.

Now let's think of this through the eyes of a police officer who deals with this kind of exposure on a continual basis. Again, from an awareness perspective, know that this job will make you susceptible to this PTSD, and when you, your friends, or loved ones notice symptoms, you need to seek help before it takes over your life.

Reducing the Stigma

Recently, law enforcement has developed strategies that focuses on officers' mental health. As one of its designs, it wants to take the stigma out of these situations. Members are now encouraged to talk about how one fatal car accident or crime scene affected them. I think this is a positive step because the more you talk about it, the more you begin to realize that other people are feeling exactly the same way. This can take a lot of pressure off you by removing that sense of isolation or weakness. As a culture, this will be a difficult transition because it is truly a different way of thinking. On one occasion, I dealt with a member who was involved in a series of unrelated events. One of those events, in and of itself, was enough to cause significant stress on this member, and it should have triggered awareness, but when combined with the other events, it compounded the stress. I spoke to this member, suggesting that some time off was needed, and my suggestion was met with resistance. The member was adamant that the time was not needed. This seems to be a natural response because, as the police, we are expected to take the bad with the good. It took some convincing, but the member finally took the time and it was for the good of everyone.

Exercise is one of the best things that you can do for yourself to help you deal with stress. The importance of looking after yourself physically and having some sort of routine, which involves consistent exercise, cannot be understated. It is amazing how much physical activity helps in your fight against stress. When you exercise, you are looking after yourself. I can recall the number of times that I worked day and night on a high-profile, exhausting investigation, and when we finally stopped, after an intense number of days, I was knocked off my feet. If I had eaten a little better and exercised a little more, then my

Remember who the important people in your life are, the people who will be there: your family and friends.

recovery time would have been minimal. During this time, I was of no use to anyone, least of all my family. I had just spent how many days away from them dealing with the file, and now, when it was all said and done, I was again away from them, as I was physically and emotionally absent while my body recovered. When you are going through this recovery phase, you cannot be selfish. Remember who the important people in your life are, the people who will be there: your family and friends. Consider how your retreating will affect them.

Focus on What Grounds You

Included in this aspect of awareness needs to be something that will ground you. Ask yourself what is important to you and your family, and where do you want your lives to take you when your career is all said and done. If you know what kind of stresses police work will place on you and, more importantly, upon your loved ones, then you can come up with strategies to make it through the difficult times. This is really a way of building resilience to accomplish this. It will always be the little things that you will remember, and they tend to be the most important when you begin to reflect on your life. Whenever possible, do not miss out on special moments like holidays, birthdays or family vacations. I think back to a time when I was posted to the Division General Investigation Section (GIS).

It was my birthday, and a tour of the first diamond mine was planned, which meant a flight out of Yellowknife. I had planned to be home at the usual time, but I must have been kidding myself. I knew that flying in the North is on its own timetable, and you land when you land. When I walked through the door, if looks could kill, I would have been a dead man. This is one of my regrets because I was just thinking that it was my birthday and I could do what I want. I did not realize that my family had planned a special birthday dinner for me and that my daughters had dressed up pretending to be a waitress and a Maître D. I remember Shantelle wearing one of my sports coats, along with a penciled moustache. Those girls waited for what seemed like forever for me. It was not about me; it was about us. That is the take away here: no matter what you are doing, no matter what accolades you may receive, it is about you and your family at the end of the day. That is a memory I will never forget, and if I had to do it all over again, I would not have taken the trip. I may have never seen a diamond mine, but the family memories of that birthday dinner would have been far more meaningful.

I believe that my family has always been my coping mechanism to help me deal with the stressors of the job. If I had understood that earlier in my career, I would have approached things a little differently, and with less regret. In his

When you decide to retire, your oasis must be intact, or you will have nothing.

book *Shifting Sands,* Steve Donahue talks about the importance of "stopping at the oasis," a metaphor for allowing yourself to recharge yourself as a means of achieving some sort of LWB. My family has always been, and *will* always be, my oasis. When you decide to retire, your oasis must be intact, or you will have nothing.

The sad thing about life is that it seems that something bad always has to happen before we get the wake-up call. I remember back in 1997, when I received the call from Chris. He told me that he had been diagnosed with stomach cancer. This cancer is ruthless, and the prognosis had no happy ending. This was my little brother, and he was in his early thirties. We should not have been having this conversation. I felt numb, and I did not know what to think. I knew one thing for sure, that I had to go to him. At the time, I was working in Yellowknife, and I made immediate arrangements to go and be with him.

A lot of things have happened since that phone call. I was thinking about him, and what he must have gone through, and the thoughts that must have been going through his head. I would imagine that there would be some kind of bargaining with a higher order. An examination of his mortality. Why does something bad always happen before something good happens? The problem I had was figuring out what the good would be in this situation.

I spoke to Chris about this time, and how he survived. When Chris was thirty years old, his life and the life of his wife Sara started changing quickly – as is typical of any couple starting a small family. The birth of their first child Katy was one of the greatest and most fulfilling experiences of his life. He doubted his ability to give her everything that she needed, not just right there and then, but years down the road. He began to worry about this, and it took its toll on him. He started getting stomach pain. The stomach pain continued to the point where he was now vomiting. The vomiting continued to the point where the inside wall of his stomach was bleeding. The bleeding, stomach pains, and vomiting were so severe that he finally went to the doctor.

After going through numerous tests, he received a phone call that summoned him and Sara to a doctor's appointment. Why would anyone think the worst? We were not brought up this way. Always look at things from a positive angle, we were taught, and everything would be alright. In Chris's mind, they simply wanted to speak to him about his diet because he was suffering from ulcers. His life changed in the blink of an eye, and there was no going back. The doctor was very blunt, telling Chris and Sara, "You have stomach cancer, and there is nothing we can do."

How do you process something like that? How do you go home and tell the rest of your family and friends that a doctor has told you that there is nothing that can be done to save your life? For Chris, there were no options. He needed to know what the next step was and how he was going to meet that challenge. Within two weeks, he was in the hospital, and after a laborious five-hour operation, they removed eighty percent of his stomach, and twenty-four lymph nodes surrounding the stomach area. Later, tests would show that the cancer had already spread to the lymph nodes. This was not a good sign. In actual fact, even with the measures taken, the doctors would only give him a prognosis of six months to live. That was in 1997.

It was then that Chris needed to start relying on the person who he really was. He fell back on our competitive blood, which he used so often in playing sports when we were growing up. There was no way this disease was going to beat him!

When you are fighting cancer, you realize that this disease has no boundaries. It can afflict anyone, at any time and, at any age. Chris came to this realization during his many trips to the cancer clinic. One week, he would be in the chair, getting his treatment, looking around and saying to himself, *I am the youngest person in here*. Then, the next week, sitting in the same chair, he found himself saying, *I am the oldest person in here*. In his mind, he began to see that, as a community, we have to do something about this disease.

It was not until one of his last trips to the cancer clinic that Sara noticed a sign on the side of the road, advertising a relay for cancer. At that moment, they knew it was something they were destined to do. This relay is now run once a year throughout communities in North America. It has been eighteen years and Chris, Sara, and their team, have raised over $140,000 and they are still as committed as if it was the first year. Chris characterizes himself as being a "cancer conqueror," rather than a cancer survivor.

> *I feel that, if you have been through doctor's appointments, operations, chemotherapy and other treatments, and the consequential side effects, and lived to tell about your journey, then you are more than a survivor, you are a CONQUEROR! For someone who has never been through something like this, simply show them your calendar, and they will know that you have been through something very intense by all the rigorous scheduling on it.*

When you hear the kind of life-changing news that my brother Chris did, it truly makes you take inventory. You ask yourself some tough questions and reflect upon what should be important in your life. What is important will be different for everyone, but we should not wait for that piece of bad news to make us realize what is most important to us. This is part of the awareness process, which will help you to move towards stability, when you get knocked off your feet.

As a cancer conqueror, I asked Chris what LWB means to him, and he shared this with me:

> *Balancing work and play becomes a priority once you have had cancer. Cancer really makes you think about what is important in life. Is it having a huge house, two cars, making lots of money, and all the big toys that come along with it? No! For us, cancer provided a new perspective on what life should be about. For us, it was being able to live in an affordable house with the focus being on spending as much time with family, as opposed*

to having to work just to keep up with material things. We feel that creating long-lasting memories with family is way more important than having material things. Once again, this is a matter of prioritizing and a simple way of thinking. Cancer has allowed us to rethink our approach on life and how we want to live it. We were lucky to have learned this at an early stage in our lives and have cancer to thank for that. Sounds odd, but never turn a blind eye to what you can learn, even from cancer. After a life-threatening illness, you learn to focus on the positives that surround you ever day. I like to tell people that it is really easy to do; it is just a simple mindset. Every situation needs to be turned around to be in your favour. It was that same philosophy that I had to rely on this past December (2013), when once again, I was diagnosed with cancer. This time, I was diagnosed with Stage 1 kidney cancer. This was very difficult for our family, as my son Rhys had a close friend whose father struggled with the same cancer for two years and lost his battle, after a valiant fight. To this day my friend, Tony Kot, gives me inspiration to live life to the fullest and to cherish every moment you have with your family.

Having a great sense of humour helped Chris to get through his ordeal. He passed this quote on to set the stage: "There is no life without humour. It can make the wonderful moments of life truly glorious, and it can make tragic moments bearable." (Rufus Wainwright). Chris has always had a great sense of humour, and there is no doubt that this helped him with his positive attitude, no matter what he has been faced with. Humour also plays a big part in dealing with the stress during the everyday job as a police officer. Often, we use the term *dark humour*. This type of humour is often viewed as morbid, cruel, graphic in nature, and can be offensive to some, but it is still found funny. As it relates to police work, I can only say that it helps to take the edge off being in a stressful environment, such as a graphic crime scene. It does not take the stress away; it only puts a lid on it for a moment. I think it is healthy in some circumstances, but you can never ignore what the continual stress of that environment is doing to you over time. Remember that, if you do, it will kick you off your ass.

When I was going through the breakup of my first marriage, I felt all alone and believed that there was no way someone could understand what I was going through. I then had a few people share their experiences with me, and it helped to put things in perspective. Just knowing that someone else had experienced something devastating in their life and survived gave me a sense of comfort and confidence that I would be able to do the same thing – and I did. I am not saying that it was not without challenges, but in the end, I got to know myself better and realized that life is to be lived.

Practice Preventative Maintenance

You also need to be realistic and acknowledge that you will likely have the wind knocked you a number of times in your life, and you will not know when or where. We all intuitively know this, but we choose to ignore it because we often think that there is no way something like that will ever happen to us. The harsh reality is that it *will* happen, and it may continue to happen if you don't take the time to build your own support strategies that include friends, families, co-workers, and professionals. You are never alone, and there is always a helping hand to get you through the rough times – reach out and grab on to it.

Always have this awareness, and think about what you need to do to prepare yourself for the road ahead. Think of it as preventative maintenance. Have the strategies in place so you can weather the storms. This does not mean that you will not be scared/scarred along the way, but these strategies will help to guarantee survival. Invest in and enjoy relationships with people who you will come to know as your family. They will be your confidants in those tough times, and if they truly know you, they will be honest with you. This may hurt you in the short term, but it will be the best for you at the end, regardless of the challenge you have been facing. Chris was kicked on his ass, not once, but twice. He came to the same conclusion that I did, namely, that family was the key.

Stress is not cancer, but it is also a silent killer. In the end, you want to be a stress *conqueror*, not just a survivor. The only way it will truly work is if all police officers band together. Look to the future and imagine a room full of conquerors, making it easier for the next generation of police officers.

Chapter Five Sound Bites
- Develop a sixth sense of awareness
- Build strong support with family in the centre
- Be a healthy barber and invest in yourself

Chapter Six
A CAREER PATH

There walks a lady we all know
Who shines white light and wants to show
How ev'rything still turns to gold...
And she's buying a stairway to heaven

"Stairway to Heaven"
—Led Zeppelin, 1971

Compete with Yourself!

The principle of abundance has been around for a long time, but its importance may be crucial in planning your career path. On the other hand, you may wish to subscribe to the principle of scarcity. This principle rests on the premise that the opportunities are limited. As a result, you will find that this will increase the competitive nature in work environments, where multiple individuals are vying for the same job. There is nothing wrong with being competitive, given that there is so much development that can come out of a healthy competitive environment. When it comes to career advancement, I have preferred to compete only with myself. In other words, I have challenged myself to get better every day. You may laugh as it sounds so Canadian, but at the end of the day, if I was not successful in getting the position I was applying for, I believed it was because I was not the best person for the job. I was not the best person for the job because I had not put in the amount of effort required so that the managers analyzing my track record could come to another conclusion.

In the selection process, you need to put aside those cases where an individual gets a job over you because of who they know – or for some other political reason. This may appear to happen, time and time again, but I would suggest that the frequency is relatively low in the bigger scheme of job selection because, at the end of the day, the organization really wants the best person for the job. Unfortunately, when this type of nepotism happens, it is not good for the morale of the masses and only serves to perpetuate the "Old Boys Club" mentality.

Go in with Your Eyes Wide Open

The interesting thing about this is that, when you do any reading about being a successful leader, you will find that you are supposed to surround yourself with people who have strong skill sets in order to guarantee your success. I am not sure about you, but if I personally know someone who has that capability, and I work well with them, then common sense would dictate that I would select them. They must have the requisite attributes or there should be no further consideration given to their application. It is a question of whether your glass is half empty or half full. If you believe that there are plenty of promotions or transfers going around, and you focus on what you want, then at one point you will get that next move. There are exceptions to this of course. There can only be one Prime Minister, one Chief of Police, or one Commissioner. This is the reality of choosing your career path, and depending on where you are in your career, this will dictate when you have to deal with the potential limitations of advancement. If your goal is to become the Chief of Police, know that your chances are extremely limited and that the competition will be fierce. You have to go into it with your eyes wide open.

If you have the belief that there are plenty of opportunities for everyone, then this helps to put your mind in the right head space when you think about your chances for success. This is especially true in an organization such as the RCMP. With thirty thousand members, plus or minus, you can easily choose from several disciplines and locations across Canada. I have kept my ear to the ground to find out what is happening out there career-wise, not so much for myself, but for the younger generation. Having a conversation with an old colleague confirmed what I have been thinking. In my day, you chose to work for one organization, and you were there from day one until retirement. That was your career path – simple, plain, and practical. I am not sure whether it was based on loyalty or some other factor I cannot seem to put my finger on. By contrast, the Millennials will have multiple careers. The single career aspect will still be alive in the future, but never to the same extent that it has been.

With this in mind, if you are going to move from one job to another, the strategy is that you move up or across, but not down. This means that you find a job doing the same kind of work that you are doing on a higher wage scale, and you continue this process throughout your working years. These same types of opportunities are available to you in police work. There are so many different career paths that you can take, while still working for the same organization. You can work the front line, move into major crime followed by forensics, and then you can find yourself in behavioural sciences. I could go on and on as the possibilities are almost endless.

This presents a dichotomy when it comes to the principle of abundance. As you advance in your career, there will be some jobs where this principle will hold no water. Securing the next promotion may depend on your networking ability, or it may simply be pure luck. In one instance, I applied for a job that would have been perfect for my career advancement. I contacted our Human Resources Staffing people, only to find that I was the only applicant. I thought that it was a sure win, but that was not the case. There was another individual who slipped into the position because it was deemed a priority transfer. What does that mean, I wondered? It simply meant that the individual's position no longer existed and they had to be moved somewhere else, or because of their personal situation, that job would be the one that best fit their needs. When this door closed, another quickly opened for me, and it turned out to be the best move I had made at the time.

Understand Your Competencies

A competency is the combination of observable and measurable knowledge, skills, abilities, and personal attributes.

If this was you first day on the job then, where would you begin? How do you decide what your path is going to be? In order to determine this, you need to understand the context in which the business you are working for operates. I have used the word business here because the context is competencies. It is not only the police that have adopted the use of competencies to measure their employees' abilities for both development and selection for promotion. You must understand what a competency is and what it means to you as far as being successful in your career path. A competency is the combination of observable and measurable knowledge, skills, abilities, and personal attributes. There are usually several levels of proficiency associated with a competency. Each level has specific criteria that allow you to determine where you are and then derive a development plan in order to get to the next level. The bottom level is very basic, whereas the top level is mastering that competency to the point where you are able to teach others how to perform the skill set or ability. On the front line of policing, you may focus on the ability to interview and interrogate, and then look at the levels of proficiency that are associated with that competency. Most organizations will have competency dictionaries that provide examples of the knowledge, skills, or abilities associated with the different levels of proficiency.

The RCMP has two categories of competencies: one is functional, and the other is organizational. The latter is really based on your ability to influence change in the organization, whereas the former focuses on individual development. There are some crossover ones that speak to both, such as networking and relationship building. You need to network and build relationships at all levels, so this might be one to start honing right from the start. It will certainly serve you well later in your career.

Remain Flexible

When starting to develop the functional competencies, you must also have a clear understanding of how the organizational ones fit into the grand scheme of things as this will be important to your future success. Once you have a handle on what the competencies mean in the various lines of police work, then start to think about your career path. You need to be flexible here, depending on your location or branch of the organization. This means that you should select competencies that will prepare you for more than one path at a time. It is somewhat similar to declaring a major or minor in university; there will be courses that will be constants or, if you will, pre-requisites. For example, if you were to look at drug enforcement and major crime, you would find that there are several competencies required by both streams if you are to achieve success. These include, but are not limited to: interviewing and interrogation, the ability to obtain judicial authorizations (search warrants), and the ability to handle confidential informants. These are great competencies to focus your development efforts on because they are also applicable to general duty (uniform) work.

The skill sets that you want to develop are no different than they were when I started police work. The difference now is that there is a more structured approach that clarifies expectations and provides opportunities to better plan your development of these skills. Another important competency that you will need to pay attention to is the ability to understand knowledge of applicable laws and legislation. As I have already mentioned, one of the most important habits you can develop is reading case law. I know that most would see reading case law as a cure for insomnia, but from a practical standpoint, a strong knowledge will allow you make better informed decisions during the course of your investigations.

There is case law with respect to everything that the police have done during investigations. It speaks to interview and interrogation, searches with and without a warrant, impaired driving, and the interception of private communication (wiretap). Regardless of what the case is, and regardless of what your

One of the most important habits you can develop is reading case law.

investigation is, it will be applicable to what you are doing. The joy of case law, from a best-practices perspective, is that the courts have just played "armchair quarterback" with your investigation, telling you what you have done well and what you have done poorly in the context of the law. You want to pay more attention to the negative because the courts are sending a message to the police regarding their expectation for future conduct.

In the first instance where the courts have identified an area where they believe the police are offside in their investigations, the evidence is still generally let in after a Section 24(2) analysis. This is a Charter (*Canadian Charter of Rights and Freedoms*) analysis to determine whether the evidence should be allowed, based on the nature of the offence and the "foul" that the police have committed. It helps to establish the rules of engagement for police investigations, but the challenge with this is that the playing field, or decisions, are always changing. Reading case law helps you keep up-to-date.

Understand Both the Criminal Code and Provincial Statutes

Understanding both case law and statute law is important as it relates to the competency of the ability to conduct investigations. On the front line, this means understanding both the *Criminal Code* and provincial statutes. I see so many police officers lacking in this area, and yet it is one of the most important. Developing this understanding opens so many doors. If you understand the offence you're investigating, then this helps to guide your investigation. It guides the investigation because if you understand the offence, you understand what evidence is necessary to prove the elements of the offence. If you understand the evidence that is needed to prove the elements of an offence – and support a charge that the Crown is willing to prosecute – then you will be able to develop investigative strategies that will gather the evidence to support the charges.

I once heard that investigating a homicide is no different than investigating a break and enter, and to some degree, that is correct. The foundation is understanding the elements of the offence. The strategies that will result and the techniques that are used will be up to you or your investigative team. What this will mean to you, and what it meant to me when I was practicing Law Enforcement, is that you need to open the *Criminal Code* and look at the possible offences you could be investigating.

As a concrete example, let's look at a break and enter as a good example to demonstrate this. You can find this in Section 348 of the *Criminal Code* of Canada:

Meeting Operational Objectives

OFFENCE: Section 348(1) CC:

Everyone who (a) breaks and enters a place with intent to commit an indictable offence therein, (b) breaks and enters a place and commits an indictable offence therein, or (c) breaks out of a place after (i) committing an indictable offence therein, or (ii) entering the place with intent to commit an indictable offence therein, is guilty (d) if the offence is committed in relation to a dwelling-house, of an indictable offence and liable to imprisonment for life, and (e) if the offence is committed in relation to a place other than a dwelling-house, of an indictable offence and liable to imprisonment for a term not exceeding ten years or of an offence punishable on summary conviction.

ELEMENTS: 1) Identification;
2) Break & Enter;
3) Place;
4) Commit
Indictable offence:

MEETING	1) ID of Suspect:	3) Place:
ELEMENTS:	Evidence to prove element:	Evidence to prove element:
	Fingerprints, confidential	Victim Statement.
	informant information,	
	video surveillance,	4) Commit offence:
	Cautioned statement	Evidence to prove element:
		Victim Statement.
	2) Break & Enter:	
	Evidence to prove element:	
	Victim Statement,	
	Fingerprints	

Once you have completed this inventory, you will see what is left over, and this is where you will focus your investigation. In most cases, it will be identification. You will likely have a good idea who is responsible for the crime, but you need to place that individual at the crime scene. I do not know how many times I have said that it takes thirty seconds to solve a crime, but proving it, well that is another ball game altogether. The other ball game entertains the process that I am explaining to you. Once you get in the habit of reading the *Criminal Code,* your degree of success will start to increase. You will be on to the next break and enter, but you must start exactly the same way, by reading the offence. In fact, each and every time you get called to a complaint of a break and enter, you should read what the *Criminal Code* says is necessary to demonstrate that an offence has occurred. This is a great habit to develop. It is akin to being a pilot. Before takeoff, a pilot has a set routine that must be followed in order to ensure the safety of all on board, and the takeoff does not occur until this check has been completed. The reason you need to complete a check similar to the pilot's is that, as much as you will understand what the *Criminal Code* is telling you, what you will not immediately understand is what this means in the context of your investigation or your case facts. These will be different every time. If you conduct your investigation in line with what I have advised, the stage will be set for your interview plan because you know the crime inside and out, not to mention the background(s) of the individual(s) whom you have arrested.

The Link to Competencies

All of these activities are consistent with what officers have done for generations, but as I have mentioned, you become more aware of their significance when you link them to competencies. The great thing about working uniform policing is that, simply by the nature of the investigations, you will be exposed to a number of competencies. Once you have a handle on developing yourself in a competency or two, this will become part of your learning plan. You need to have a development plan. All police agencies have learning plans attached to their annual assessments. This was done with the best of intentions, but it seemed that it was a "check the box" kind of exercise and really did not result in what it needed to be. This is likely because it was imposed rather than someone having the desire and motivation to develop. Take a few of these competencies and make them the focus of your learning plan. You do not have to wait a year to develop your next plan. A learning plan, like a good CV, will be a living document.

Once you have developed yourself to a desired level in a competency, you can go to the next level or choose another competency. The great thing about this is that it is your choice. Just let it happen naturally. I spoke to an officer once who had a hobby of being validated on as many competencies as possible. Validation occurs when a board convenes and reviews competency examples. Their job is to judge whether the example is at the level it needs to be for that particular job. In a perfect world, you would just naturally validate at levels as you invest in your development as a police officer. Too often, I have seen members say they need to develop an example for a given competency. That is the problem with *any* system. People will try and figure it out and make it work and take short cuts. You are not doing yourself or the people you are going to be supervising any favours if you take this tack. Keep in mind the principle of abundance. I have mentioned that I chose not to compete for promotion until later in my service, when I was ready. Because of this, I was more than capable of doing the job and then some, and this is where you want to be.

S.T.A.R. – Situation, Task, Action, and Response

When it comes to writing these documents it is all about you, not we.

There will come a point where you will have to be practical when it comes to promotion to ensure that, when you put your name in the hat for consideration, you have made the best impression that you can with your track record as a police officer. This means developing a reputation for yourself as a strong investigator right from the call to the conviction. It will depend on the protocol for promotion. For each job, there is what is called a competency profile. The profile lists the competencies associated to the job. Generally, you will see both organizational and functional competencies, but for the purpose of early promotion, the focus is on the functional competencies. You will then provide two examples for each competency. This can be a challenge for some people, especially those who do not like to blow their own horn. The fact is that you will have to get over this because we are talking about your career. You don't do your development any favours if you have not taken the time to develop yourself or are unable to demonstrate this. Typically, the examples are written using the S.T.A.R. format (Situation, Task, Action, and Response), but what is most important in this format that you articulate your *role* in the situation. Once you have established that, then you must painstakingly say exactly what you did and break it down into steps. What you are really doing is showing is how your actions influenced the outcome. Generally speaking, the higher level of promotion will have a larger span of influence that needs to be reflected in your answers. As much as police work takes place in a team environment, when it comes to writing these documents, it is all about *you*, not we.

The validation board and the line manager who is selecting you does not care what your team has done, they are more interested to know what you did for your team that caused the team to have that great result. It could be a dynamic entry into a house during the execution of a search warrant that you planned, instructed, monitored and gave feedback as to how things unfolded, which resulted in development for all members of your team. Do not be afraid to talk to colleagues when trying to scare up some of these examples. Chances are you have a repertoire, but you just don't realize it. I think those officers that just do the job for the love of the job have the most trouble with this because they are not thinking competency; they are thinking about doing the job and doing it well. They are doing themselves a disservice, however; because they are not paying attention to all the great examples.

It's helpful to keep a journal for this purpose. This is a notebook where you would just jot a few lines to aid in memory when drafting your examples. It should be done daily because, before you know it, you are on to your next and forget about that great example that you experienced last week. Do not be afraid to go to senior officers who have gone through the system and get them to read your examples. Take the advice with a grain of salt. The reason that I am saying this is that when it comes to a validation board, there is a strong element of subjectivity. As much as the senior officer's opinion is important and relevant, the board might see it in a different light. You will still get some good pointers, but what is more important is that you talk about *yourself* and what influence you brought to the given examples that caused a positive result.

Once your confidence as a police officer begins to develop along with your skill set, I would suggest that you volunteer to assist with the validation boards. It gives you an appreciation of how the system works and puts you in a better place to help others. There will be some things you will not be able to share with others because of confidentiality, but you can certainly discuss process. In a perfect world, everyone would understand the process and format equally so that they would all be on the same playing field. The only consideration would be to pick the best person for the job because the examples would really shine through. There would be no guessing what the individual did in the situation.

Stretch Yourself

Aside from your everyday work in your efforts to follow your career path, it is always important to have a project on the side of your desk. Call this a stretch assignment and it is meant purely for your development. It stretches your ability to a different level. You should choose something that is not overly taxing but still serves your development needs. It may be something as simple as sitting on a committee where you contribute to change either within your organization or outside – or both. An example of this is becoming part of a team. At one point in my service, they were looking for people to form an interview team. This team would be called upon to assist with interviews/interrogations for high-profile investigations and/or high-profile criminals. I volunteered for this, and it no doubt contributed substantially to my development in this competency. Another example is a Health and Safety committee. I am not telling you that you need to do this to be successful, but it helps. It will depend on you and your abilities to take on something over and above. Always know your limits, and do not take on more than you can handle, or *everything* suffers.

Choose Your Career Path Carefully

Understanding what a career path is and taking the time to carefully choose what yours will be is truly where you will find job satisfaction.

You can see over time that you will have developed yourself in a number of competencies associated with the career path you wish to take. As you travel on in your career, you will come to a fork in the road, and you will take one path or the other. Each road will have competencies that the other will not. In either case, you will need to entertain the same process of developing yourself at different levels of the competencies. The great thing about police work is that, if you choose one path and it is not the right one, all you have to do is back up the truck and take the other road. Over time, you will have built a strong foundation of policing skills, so it will not matter that much. It is almost re-inventing yourself but in a different police discipline. Understanding what a career path is and taking the time to carefully choose what yours will be is truly where you will find job satisfaction. But never forget that, while travelling that path, you must take people with you. Take only those that want to go, and leave the door open for others. The ones that do not want to go may not be ready or may be looking to follow a different path.

One of the challenges I have both experienced and witnessed in this regard is the level of expectation. Once you have done something really well, you will receive some accolade, but this wears off pretty quick and it doesn't take long for the "what have you done for me *lately*" feeling to rear its ugly head. I guess this is a double-edged sword because, truly, you do want to get better each and every time, but it should fall in line with your expectations and your development.

Chapter Six Sound Bites
- Opportunities for success are everywhere
- Choose the path with multiple forks
- Learn the basics and constantly push yourself to a higher level

Chapter Seven
RELATIONSHIPS

He said I was finally the husband,
That most the time I wasn't.
And I became a friend a friend would like to have ...

"Live Like You Were Dying"
—Tim McGraw, 2004

The Importance of Commitment

As people, we really cannot survive without interaction with others. It is our nature, and it's how we've survived from generation to generation. Relationships make us whole and give our lives meaning. They come in a variety of forms and can last seconds or years. This is part of the magic of relationships. It does not matter how long the relationship lasts for it to have impact or influence the way you live and appreciate your own life. Most of the time, we really don't appreciate the power of these relationships. In all relationships, commitment is the constant element. This is another life lesson that Dad taught me and not by design. He had the innate ability to talk to perfect strangers, and before you knew it you could hear his infectious laugh. He was a great listener and showed sincerity when he was talking to you no matter who you were. He had a sense of calmness that made it comfortable for anyone to talk to him. I thought it was just because he was my dad that I had this feeling when being around him until I had a conversation with Bob after he had passed. Bob, his only son-in-law, told me that he felt exactly the same way. I think people reacted this way to him only because he expected nothing in return. This does not mean that return in a relationship is not important, but it has to be put in the right perspective. No matter who it is, you have to be committed to that person or group, and it will be that degree of commitment that will be a measure of how important that relationship is to you. That degree of commitment will also have a direct influence on the return in that relationship.

Another important element in this mix is sincerity. If it is a true relationship, you will be sincere with your interactions. This will also have bearing on the return in your relationship. Return is a funny thing; it can either be by design or chance. I would think that the returns of chance will have the most impact and meaning for you. Even business relationships that are more clinical can result in enduring personal relationships.

No matter where you work, when you show up for your first day, your feelings will be the same. It will be uneasy at first, but you will begin to get to know people and feel comfortable. You will know who you can trust and who can help you with your day-to-day tasks. You will begin to understand who you want to get to know to help you learn a new skill and who you want to get to know to give you career advice. You will get to know those people who you want to develop personal relationships with. It does not matter which of these relationships you are looking to form because you must approach them all the same way.

Be Yourself and Be Sincere

You need to be yourself and be sincere, despite how hard it may be for you or how vulnerable it may make you feel. In order to develop a true relationship, you have to be both of these things. Just as importantly, you must show commitment to people. This will come in different ways and will depend on the task or conversation at hand for you to choose how much of a relationship you want to have with these people. Do not try to force these relationships, let them happen naturally. Know that all people tick the same way, and we really do want to help each other, but keep your eyes wide open for those who are just passing through and will use you for their own benefit. If you do this with every person you meet with varying degrees, it will be amazing the people you can talk to.

When you get comfortable doing this in your work environment, take the same tack with your external partners. I am not asking that you be a social butterfly, just do it at your comfort level; that is all that anyone can ask for. Do not compromise this and treat people differently. As a supervisor, you may have to choose someone for a job that you do not have the best relationship with, but your job is to pick the best person for the job regardless how you feel about them personally. If you take inventory of yourself with respect to your impartiality, it will enhance your ability to interact with people. If you are really lucky, then you may have developed a couple of strong confidants and even the odd personal relationships. We really are in the same boat and trying to get to the same island, and there is plenty of island for everyone. It is much nicer to be on an island paradise with the people we love and care about than being stranded there alone. Know that relationships are important and that you have to commit and work at them each and every day of your life. They will also vary depending on where you are in your career or life.

Early in my service, my trainer told me that I needed to get on the reserve (Sturgeon Lake Indian Reserve #154) and bang on a different door every day. I did and got to know the people better than a lot of other members. It helped me to do my job on more than one occasion and probably saved me from some tight situations. Police work is a people business, and you need to develop relationships with people in order to survive. This is just a given. Today it is all about networking and who you know in order to get your job done or, depending on your aspirations, how to advance your career. If you are a good networker and put yourself in the right position, then you stand the chance of getting the next promotion. Just know that developing relationships or networking is vital to your success as a police officer.

Partner Relationships

In this vein, the *types* of relationships need to be understood. You have your personal relationships that are outside of your day-to-day work. You have external relationships where natural partnerships have occurred over your time with the police, who include government officials, Crown, doctors and nurses. These are the people who you need to interact with just to get the job done. The partner relationships will vary depending on where you are working. What about the people who make you look good, the support staff? These are the people that really make the office go around. They include guards, stenos, office managers, assistants and janitorial staff. One of the most important pieces of advice that I received when I left Depot Division (RCMP Training academy) was how important it is to develop relationships with these people. These people will be the constant in the office, and they keep the ship on an even keel. You need to get to know them quickly and really understand how important they are to you and your development. Consider your relationship with your fellow officers. There will always be a pecking order both formally and informally, and you need to know how you fit in this hierarchy as it will influence how you interact with your colleagues. Formally, you will have those officers that have higher ranks and hold supervisor positions at various levels and then you will have those who are at the same rank as you but will have more time in the Force and, because of this, may *unofficially* outrank you. Inevitably, you will have crossover personal relationships with some of the people in one or several of these groups. These are two different types of relationships where you really need to understand the boundary. In my first posting, one corporal's wife was hired as office staff, and they saw each other both during the workday and then at home. I couldn't imagine the challenge that may have posed. I am sure the same could be said for two officers who are living together.

The other type of relationship you'll be developing will be with your clients on the street. In these relationships, you have to understand that a lot of these people do not have nice lives and have not been treated with respect or kindness. The key to success here is to treat them no differently than anyone else with whom you have a relationship, which means with the same degree of commitment and sincerity. What makes it easy in a sense is that there will be a natural boundary that must be respected for several different reasons. This is a professional relationship, and there cannot be a personal relationship. This must be made clear and there can be no misconceptions.

Boundaries Must Be Set and Respected

I have the feeling I'm stating the obvious again but with reason. Early in my service, a junior member began to develop an informant. The informant was of the opposite sex and a minor. As time went on, lines were crossed and the member became involved personally. Think about the damage all around because it affects both of these people on so many levels. On a personal level because there were no doubt emotions involved, on a professional level because this was far from professional (yet it developed *from* a professional relationship) and more importantly on moral and ethical levels, which would have a rippling affect with respect to how the public view the police.

Needless to say, this member did not stay in the Force long, nor did that relationship last. Boundaries are important and need to be respected in relationships. There is too much at stake. Some of the front-line clients might be the less than desirable people, but if you regularly stop and chat with them, they may be the ones who reach out to you and provide significant insight when you are faced with an investigation. What you talk about is no different than what you discuss when you first meet people – small talk. You talk about the weather, sports, and music. I always found that humour is great to develop relationships. You need to make them laugh. In fact, humour in any of your relationships can solidify that relationship for life. You will just never know how much they mean to you or touch your life, but there are things that happen that remind us how important they really are. Like an old cliché, we don't realize how much they meant to us until they are gone. Just think of your own life; I'm sure you will find something that will bring what I am saying to life.

I had just pulled off the highway after another long commute, and I got the call from Ray. I had not talked to him in a bit, and it was good to hear his voice. Something was different this time, and there was an awkward silence and then I heard the words, "Les is dead." It took me a few seconds to process what I had just heard. Les had passed away of a heart attack at the age of fifty. Les lived in Nova Scotia, and we lived on the other side of the country, and Ray asked me if I would go to the funeral with him. This is when the negotiation started. It was not with Ray; it was with me. I was trying to rationalize with myself that it was too far and how I could not afford it. Then my head arrived where it should have been. This man had meant so much to me and had such an impact on my life. I had spent too much time pondering this decision that should have been an easy *yes* from the start. In no time, we were on the east coast and were honoured to be pallbearers. Ray, thanked me after our trip. There is nothing better to help you deal with the death of an old friend than being with another old friend.

You see my relationship with Les evolved out of happenstance. I was working on an unsolved homicide in the Northwest Territories in a settlement on the Mackenzie River. I had worked on it for some time, and Les was brought on board because of his knowledge and relationship with the community. I was still wet behind the ears and figured I could learn something from this seasoned vet. He worked on this homicide and later another with me. During the second investigation, we actually lived together for a year and became great friends. Ray had a similar working experience with Les.

What Are You Thinking?

My time with Les taught me two very important things that have shaped not only my career but me as a person. The first was the realization that we cannot read minds and that strong communication is the most important trait you can develop as a person. That realization happened by chance during the time I was just getting to know Les. Les had been posted to the settlement in the past, and knew the community inside out. We were having dinner at the corporal's residence (the man who was in charge of the detachment). It was in the middle of winter and dark, dark, dark.

Les decided he was going for a ride. I knew I could learn a lot from him and his knowledge of the community. We hopped in the police Suburban, and he gave me a tour of the settlement. I sat there and thought, *How can I tap into this knowledge in the quickest way possible?* I simply asked him, "What are you thinking?" He began to tell me about his time policing in the settlement and who was who in the community. I had intimately known the case facts, and hearing this background was priceless. It would help later with investigative strategies. Those four words: "What are you thinking?" would serve me for years to come. It doesn't matter who you're with or what setting you're in, be it at home or work; if you're working with one or more people you have to know what they are thinking, and *how* they are thinking, to increase your chances of success. I think this move achieves some kind of synergy, and if you continually work with these people over time, you will have a highly-motivated, highly-functional team.

Ya But …

The second epiphany I had was a life lesson that Les shared with me. It was the time we worked in a settlement south of Yellowknife for a year. We had set up shop in a modular home that had a kitchen, two bedrooms, a bathroom, and a living room. The living room would serve as our office, and we had two desks. We slept on the floor during this time. Like any unsolved homicide, we began with a file review to not only get to know the case facts but to develop investigative strategies. Early into this, Les took a sheet of lined paper and wrote "Ya But…" on it and placed it on the wall. It was not a "What are you thinking?" moment but more "Why are you doing this?" Les explained that *ya buts* always get in the way of getting things done. They need to be ignored in order to move things forward.

This was a motivational poster for us to keep our eyes on our goals. The homicide remains unsolved, but Les and I brought it to a new level, and we did not let any *ya buts* get in our way. *Ya buts* are easy, they are a dime a dozen, and if you listen to them, you will never be successful. Any challenge will have obstacles; it is the nature of dealing with people. It is a question of commitment. If you say *yes* to a challenge, there are no *ya buts*. This does not mean that you say yes to everything because there has to be a balance. The point is that the *ya buts* will get in the way of getting *anything* done and will certainly stunt your development.

Then There's the Humour Factor

A partner relationship is complemented well with humour now and again. Bob, my partner on the homicide unit, and I were working on an unsolved homicide and found ourselves in beautiful downtown California. We landed in San Diego and rented a car that would take us to a small town just north of San Diego. It was not just hot, it was sweltering. Bob chose to drive while I started an inventory of all the car's gadgets. We hit the highway, and I looked down and noticed the car had heated seats with separate controls for each seat. I took the liberty of turning Bob's to high as we continued down the highway. Bob is bald, but he wears it well. Sweat began to appear on his head, first the little drops and then the big ones. He began to drink water. I can't remember how long I went on with this before I let the cat out of the bag. I laughed pretty hard, and Bob was relieved because he thought he had a fever. That is only one example of using humour to develop a relationship. Try going to Dick's Last Resort in San Diego; that is good for a couple of memories and a stronger relationship at the end of the day. I will tell that story some other time.

At times during my career, if you walked into my office you would see a sign. The sign read, "The more I think about it, old Billy was right; let's kill all the lawyers, kill em tonight..." – lyrics from an Eagles song. The most important external relationship that you will have as a police officer is your relationship with the Crown, and you may even develop strong personal relationships with these people if you let yourself. There were a number of great things I learned early in my service that helped me along the way and this was one of them. After gaining some confidence in my abilities as a police officer, I was tasked with being the Court Officer. Court was held once a week in this community, and it was something of a travelling roadshow. The judge, Crown, and defence counsel would travel in from another city for court. This was a busy place, and it did not take long for your morning to be consumed before it was lunchtime. You would share this time with defence lawyers and Crown, and from *that*, great relationships would spark. You could then later call these Crown lawyers for advice, and that rapport made it so much easier when you were trying to advance investigations. More often than not, the collaboration would lead to a better investigation at the end of the day.

Working Well with Crown Counsel

Now back to the lyrics that reference Shakespeare. If we did not have the lawyers – or the law for that matter – it would be so easy to solve crime. We commonly refer to this as the pre-Charter days. Not to say that there was bad or corrupt police work being done as a practice, but the rules of engagement were quite different. I can honestly say that if I were to put in a Crown report the person committed the crime. The point is the Canadian Charter of Rights and Freedoms has to been considered in addition to other evolving case law by which the police need to consider when conducting their investigations. The Crown is instrumental in keeping the police in check as it relates to their conduct in the context of the Charter.

As much as Crown lawyers are seen as roadblocks, and cause you anguish and grief, they have your best interest at heart. You need to understand this and listen intently to what you are being told. This does not mean that you need to follow all of their direction, although you would be crazy not to. The point is

Do not be afraid to engage and question the instruction in a diplomatic manner so you really understand the direction.

do not be afraid to engage and question the instruction in a diplomatic manner so you really understand the direction. This will result in two things: you will have a better understanding of the law and you will have sound investigations using the law as one of your guiding principles. You will also begin to develop that relationship with the Crown. They are more than willing to help you. They understand their return by developing that relationship with you; you may end up with a lifelong friend. What is interesting about these relationships is that you will begin by bouncing ideas about work and investigations, which eventually lead these conversations to move to family and common interests, which strengthens that bond.

The years then start to sneak up on you, and before you know it, you're having conversations about weddings, babies, and holidays. The conversations about work become less and more personal, but then you begin to have the tough conversations. These rest on discussions of death, divorce, and any other crisis that may be going on in your life. It really does not matter what the conversation is after you have it with that friend; you have a sense of direction, and at times, the weight of the world falls off your shoulders. What if it was just one person that you had as a friend, and that person was the best friend a friend would like to have? This is a return that you never expected, but it begins with making that commitment. Always remind yourself that you cannot get to where you want to be all by yourself. You will need people in your life to help you along the way. While you are reminding yourself, keep in mind that these people that you have developed relationships with are doing the exact same thing that you are doing. They have goals and want to go places in life, and they too know they cannot do it alone. Some understand this while others develop these relationships not knowing their benefits. At the end of the day, it matters not because it is the resulting relationship that matters once you have reached that place you want to be in your life.

Always remind yourself that you cannot get to where you want to be all by yourself. You will need people in your life to help you along the way.

Along the way you will also run into people who will have a strong working relationship with you, but it will remain more clinical than personal. These people can be great to work with, but they do not understand or care about the personal aspect of relationships and see working with you as a means to moving ahead. This is not a bad thing, this is just the way that they tick. I have come across a few like that, and you can usually see them coming a mile away. They are usually pretty good at what they do, and you can certainly learn something from them. Don't get emotionally attached to them; they will just break your heart. They are like those puppies you see in the pet store. Puppies lose their cuteness pretty quickly, and some people do as well.

It reminds me of that Bob Seger song "Night Moves" and specifically the lyrics "...and we'd steal away every chance we could, to the backroom, to the alley or the trusty woods, I used her, she used me. But neither one cared..." There is nothing *wrong* with this type of relationship. The return is questionable because this person could be a great resource to call years down the road when you need something to get the job done. Given the context of your relationship with this person, they may or may not help you. You just never know. That is why you ought to approach all relationships the same way – because you just never know.

As you get transferred or move on to new units over the years, the process of building relationships continues. After years of experience, you understand the

How you grow will be up to you.

importance of these relationships. You will be able to read people better and figure out right away what kind of relationship you want to have with people in your new work environment. It is funny, and I say it again and again – we never *really* graduate from high school from a relationship point of view. In every organization, you will have the nerds, the jocks, the in crowd, and the out crowd. I think that the only difference is that, on an adult level, we somehow know how to interact with the different groups on a more mature level, allowing us to develop great working relationships with all groups of people. It is natural for you to gravitate to people who are like you. You get a sense of comfort, and it makes it easier for you to get your job done. In any event, you may even develop personal relationships with someone who is not like you, and this can make you grow as a person. How you grow will be up to you.

Chapter Seven Sound Bites:
- It is not a relationship unless you are engaged 100%
- Relationships are not finite and will evolve
- Be a friend to everyone

Chapter Eight
ADVERSITY

When you're lost
On a stormy ocean being tossed
I'll swim to you at any cost ...
I'll help you find a way around
When you're down

"Lost"
—Jimmy Rankin, 2011

Keep Your Eye on the Prize

Ever since I was a kid, I put all my heart and soul into becoming a Mountie. It was my goal, my passion, and I would do anything to make it happen, and I did. The fact that I was not successful after my first interview was no deterrent. My resolve and motivation were strong, and this was just a small detour. I needed life experience. My plan was to attend college for a year, be interviewed again, complete my basic training at Depot, and hit the streets policing in one of our beautiful provinces or territories. I soon found out that timing is everything. During that period, the recruiting criteria had changed. It was the advent of Employment Equity. If you were a woman, Indigenous, or had a university degree, you were in a better position to be hired. Being neither female nor Indigenous, I was left with only one option: to get a university degree. Nothing was going to stop me from taking the steps I had to take to make my dream come true. I chuckled to myself because I had made no plans for higher education. I just wanted to ride in a cruiser and chase the bad guys. In my Grade 12 year, I had negotiated my way out of high school, promising the teachers I had no plans to go to university. I was going to have to become something I was not in order to fulfil my lifelong dream: an academic.

Once I made the decision, I had no problem finding the motivation to work at completing my degree. I learned to be a student. I figured out what a GPA was and how important it was to have a high one. In all the years I was chasing that degree, I always kept my eyes on the prize. I was going to be a Mountie, no matter what it took. It was the best thing that ever happened to me.

Upon completion of my degree, I was interviewed again and found myself at Depot in July of 1987. My dream had become a reality. From day one, it was all excitement and fun. Getting up and going to work was no effort. If you truly love what you do, then you will never truly "go to work." This was the way I approached my job, and the opportunities and adventures were endless, the sky was the limit.

If you truly love what you do, then you will never truly "go to work."

When Real Life Kicks You Where It Really Hurts

I was foolish to think that the motivation that got me through the front door would help me get out the back one. It will be the challenges in either your work or personal life that will take the wind out of your sails. In my case, it happened after fifteen years of blood, sweat, and tears. The moon and the stars were beginning to align. I was a member of an investigative team, playing a major role, looking to solve a homicide. It was exciting being a real detective. All the years of practice could now be used and it was going to be fun. I could not wait to get to work in the morning so that I could make the next move. What was even more exciting was being able to do those things you see on TV and in the movies, things like wiretaps and undercover operations. My days were like episodes out of *The Wire*. *The Wire* was a TV show based on drug investigations, and it characterized the use of wiretap as an exciting means to catch the bad guys. It was truly like living in the movies, and there was nothing better than a good murder mystery.

Everything seemed to be perfect, then all of a sudden, my personal life began to fall apart. The house and family that I had worked so hard to have was crumbling before my eyes. Life was not *supposed* to be this way. When you marry someone, it is supposed to be for life. It was like being kicked right in the balls and having my life sucked right out of me. I was right in the middle of moving into a new house that was being renovated, while we were living in the basement. I found that I had endless energy. I would work my usual shift, and then I would paint at night, and I would hit the repeat button for the next day. Things got to the point where I had to leave the home I had worked so hard to obtain because my relationship with my wife had changed so much. I had no idea where was I going to go and what I was going to do. I honestly thought that I was on top of the world at home – and I was abruptly kicked to below sea level.

It was an emotional blow that I needed to deal with quickly because I was not going to let this affect the biggest opportunity of my career thus far. The problem with that line of thinking is that there is no such thing as a quick fix when a marriage and family are falling apart right before your eyes. I managed to find a place to stay for a short time. I then went to Pat, a friend, and asked if I could stay with him. He did not hesitate in saying yes. There I was, a man close to turning forty, living in a twelve-by-twelve tennis shack. I still had to drag myself to work, and do the best that I could.

For the first time that I could remember, I had to make myself get up and go to work. I still enjoyed the job, but I worked hard to put all my emotions aside when I walked through the door so that I could focus on what needed to be done. I never thought that I would be in this position. Where was I going to find the motivation to not only go to work, but to put on my best game face each and every day *while* my personal life was falling apart? This was when I started hearing all of those pat phrases that people tend to use when you are going through a really bad time in your life. They all meant well, and perhaps even a few of them were right, but I never felt comforted. The one that got me the most was "things happen for a reason." The uncomfortable part of that was that no one could ever tell you what the reason *was* – you either had to figure that out all by yourself or pray for an epiphany. It was really no different than finding your motivation to keep on going.

You Are Not Alone

Looking back, I guess what really helped me the most was the realization that I was not the only one in the world to have experienced a marriage break-up, although it certainly *felt* that way at the start. What I did gain from this realization was the strength and courage to get up and go to work every day, while I was trying to put myself back together. Such a life experience makes you wonder how you will get through each subsequent day while constantly asking yourself where you are going to find the motivation. It is really about finding the strength and courage to keep moving on, no matter what the obstacle is in front of you. As Nietzsche wrote, "That which does not kill us, makes us stronger"[1] and I think that this is an important thing to realize when you are going through any challenge that is before you whether it is work, family, or a combination of both. So the next time that someone says that things happen for a reason, just remember that you will hopefully come out stronger at the other side.

If you truly understand that, when you have a challenge in front of you, there really is going to be blood, sweat, and tears before you reach your goal, then you are at a good starting place. I will always remember that scene from *An Officer and a Gentleman*, when Lou Gosset Jr. is trying to break Richard Geer and get him to quit. Geer is going through a bit of an attitude adjustment for getting caught with pre-polished kit. Gosset is making him do sit-ups and demands for his DOR (Discharge on Request) and Geer repeatedly says that he is not going to quit, and then the demand that matters is made. Gosset tells Geer that he is out. Geer sits up and says desperately, "I've got nowhere else to go, I've got nowhere else to go, I've got nowhere else to go." Gosset replies: "All right

---

1   Friedrich Nietzsche. Accessed at https://www.brainyquote.com/quotes/quotes/f/friedrichn101616.html

Mayo, get on your feet." In this exchange, Gosset was trying to accomplish a few things. He was trying to figure out what Geer was doing at the Academy and he was also trying to get Geer to figure out what he was doing at the Academy. The motivation in this instance was desperation.

Desperation Happens

Desperation to get somewhere else, to be a better person, in a better place – I think that this desire will resonate with each of us at some point in our life. Think about Maslow's hierarchy of needs. It starts out with the basic needs and progresses all the way up to the altruistic needs. In this case, it is needs that create the motivation, but remember that there is a difference between a need and a want. Sometimes we do not know where our motivation comes from, and it can change over time. You can collect all the latest inspirational posters you want, but some days it will just not matter, and you will need something else to keep you going. I refer to this as blind faith.

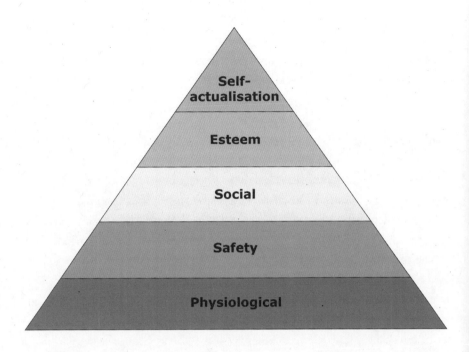

It is a trust, and to commit to this kind of trust, will depend on the person, the time, and the place. It will always be fluid because what worked yesterday may not work today. You have to understand that doing the job will impact your motivation, even to the point you may not want to get up and go to work. Trust yourself, and do not waiver, no matter what the challenge; you will get to where you want to be in the end. It's like skiing when there is a heavy cloud on the mountain and vertigo hits, you have to trust in your ability to ski. In my case, when I was going through this hard time, although I did not realize it then, the motivation was to get my self-confidence back. I had received such a blow because I had worked so hard and gone so far, only to end up with nothing.

It's always easy to play armchair quarterback, especially with your own life. I know that now because I made it through, and I am a stronger person today. I just dove in and rolled with the punches, one day at a time. At one point, I saw a glimmer of hope and really had to trust the universe because I was heading down a road that I had never been on before. It was not an untraveled road, but I was certainly proceeding with caution because I did not know where the bumps were, or how fast I could go. It was like learning to ride a bike all over again and having that wobbly front wheel on an unsteady path.

Over time, my self-confidence *did* come back. I continued to put my game face on at work, and in the end, I was successful. I did not come through without scars, but I believe that having the scars shows you are not afraid to live life. I have often said that I already know what I am going to do if this ever happens to me again. It will *not* though, for I am quite happy where I am at in my life, and with my family. As you may have already gleaned through what you have read thus far, you will find many sources of motivation to give you the kick in the ass (KITA) you need to stay on your course. As a matter of fact, sometimes all you need is a little KITA to get you going. It will not happen once, it will not happen twice, it will happen time and time again. You will not know what that spark will be to get you going, and you cannot try too hard to find it. It will come on its own, and it will work for as long as it works.

Focus on Maintenance and Momentum

This is really at the core of understanding sports and how tough it is for athletes to stay the course. It is no different as a police officer. There will be days when the world is falling apart around you, and just when you have finally made it through the day, you have to come back the next day and do it all again. The question *then* becomes "What holds us back from taking that first step?" It's just like starting a fire with friction. It takes a little while to get it started, but before you know it, the spark catches and begins to burn. It then burns brighter until the flames get higher. The moment the fire has reached this point, it is great and you never want to leave it. You are enjoying its warmth and mesmerizing beauty. It then starts to fade a bit, and you have to put another log on the fire in order to maintain its beauty. This is exactly what you want to do with yourself, and the trick will be focusing on maintenance, or keeping your momentum going. Even during times where you feel like you're spinning your wheels, you will be gaining ground and

Most of the time, we underestimate our abilities.

this is where trust and blind faith comes in once again, and it will come from your mind.

At times, our mind can be our own worst enemy. It will try to put limits on you by telling you that you cannot do this and you cannot do that. I keep telling my son, Josh, that there is no such word as *can't*. It is "limitation." So if the mind is the challenge that needs to be overcome, what is yours telling you right now? If your mind is telling you that you cannot do something, then ask yourself why. If your goal is to move from a uniform position to a plainclothes section, your mind may be telling you that you will never be able to make it – and a laundry list of reasons of why it is not possible suddenly appear:

- There are people who are better than me
- There are people more deserving
- I don't have enough service
- My family would never support me in doing something like this
- That job demands long hours and I am not sure I could balance that.

I could go on for a few pages, but I think you get the point. Now that your mind has so graciously put a number of roadblocks in front of you, there is a choice that you need to make, and the choice you make could change your life's path. Do you believe what your mind is telling you, or do you take yourself to task? We are all born equal, and born to create our own opportunities. How we pursue those opportunities is up to us.

Most of the time, we underestimate our abilities. The truth is that, not only can we do the task or job in question, we can probably do it very well. If you choose to believe what your mind is telling you, then you could be destined to be where you are for the rest of your career. A self-fulfilling prophecy is a double-edged sword. I am not saying that some of these roadblocks are unrealistic but they are roadblocks that you can find a way around.

You need to shift gears and get your mind to make another list for you to focus on as you are striving to achieve your goals. Once you have done that, then take your original NEGATIVE laundry list and come up with solutions that address the concerns. Follow up with a timeline, and then go for it. When I decided to write this book, it grew from an idea that had been cooking in my head for a few years. Finally, I committed to compiling a list of topics that I thought would be great for chapters on one of those little hotel notepads. I placed it in my shaving kit, and God knows how long it stayed there. Fast forward and eventually I started picking out song lyrics and organized them in chapter format.

One day while I was working on Vancouver Island, and having a couple of drinks with Ray, I told him I was going to write a book, but that's as far as it went. It stayed as a dormant idea until I heard Steve Donahue, a motivational speaker, speak to our group, and then I told him I was going to write a book. From that moment, I became committed to overcoming any obstacles I had placed in front of me. Once I had verbalized my intent to Steve – and a number of other people – I finally started to put words on paper. At the heart of my procrastination was my lack of self-confidence. I had never written anything like this before, and I was worried that it wouldn't be good. As you can see, I just mentioned two things that would be on my laundry list as to why I could not write a book. One was based on a lack of experience while the other had its roots in the fear of failure.

Throughout your career, holding back because you don't feel you have sufficient experience will hit you in the face again and again. There is only one way to address that and that is to do the task or components of the job over and over again until you can do it with your eyes closed. It is not easy, and it is often a humbling experience. During my service, I was posted in two provinces and a territory, and each time I moved from one to the other, I had to start all over again, no matter how much service I had. Sometimes, I did not know some of the basic laws that a six-month cadet would know, and I would have to ask. Even now that I am retired and employed outside of the RCMP, one of the most frustrating things I face is not knowing everything, and not knowing how to do it well. My advice is just get out and do it and never stop trying.

Just get out and do it and never stop trying.

Feel the Fear and Do It Anyway

On the other hand, fear can be a funny thing. It will come to us at the worst of times, and it does not matter who you are or how good you are. It can still have an adverse effect on you. Trust in your fear because it lets you know that you are human, but do not give it any power over you. When people talk about fear, it always makes me wonder what is at the heart of the fear. I have come to the conclusion that it is simply a fear of the unknown – fear of going down that untraveled road. Failure is not to be feared. It grounds us and is the motherhood of strategy, as it forces us to reflect and move forward in the direction of our goals. Of course, too much failure is not good for our egos; we all need to hit a home run now and again.

The secret, as always, is to keep swinging the bat until you connect with that ball and hit it out of the park. Each home run you hit helps to build a foundation of what you are capable of doing and building your self-confidence to take the next challenge. If you start with a goal in mind and convince yourself that you are capable of doing what it takes to reach that goal that is a great start. You then have to commit to yourself. You can think of a number of things that might make this commitment easier for you. The precise motivator does not really matter, but it needs to be something that can be sustained. Once you know what it is, do not keep it inside. You need to tell someone, and family members are usually a good place to start. At first, they may look at you questioningly, but if they love you and respect you, they will, at the very least, humour you. If you have children, be sure to tell them, no matter what their age. If they are just babies, that is perfect because they will not be judgemental.

The next step is to tell your friends and colleagues. In a sense, you are committing to all of these people that you are taking on this challenge. It may be hard to believe, but I did exactly this at the age of five. When I was asked what I wanted to be when I grew up, I replied that I was going to be a policeman, just like Dad. You should have heard the laughter. I would repeat this over and over again throughout the years and eventually, my efforts made it a reality in spite of all of the roadblocks I encountered along the way.

At one point, you have to take concrete action because it is the only thing that will truly allow you to honour your commitment, both to yourself and to others. It may also be helpful to seek others' assistance when you hit that wall – think of these people as your cheerleaders, and rely on them to give you that pep talk you need to keep going. Regardless of the challenges we are facing, we all have people backing us. One thing that I am sure of is that, once you have committed to these people, you are going to find that they will often have even more confidence in you than you will have in yourself. Keep this in mind when you find yourself in a valley, trying to find your way back to the peak. Like any good relationship, it is not the good times that will make the difference, it is when you are working through the tough times that your relationships will ultimately grow and become stronger. The same thing will happen with your self-confidence once you find your way back to the peak. Trust who you are and what you are capable of doing.

Trust who you are and what you are capable of doing.

Try Visualization

For a large number of people, visualization can be helpful. If your goal is to run a marathon, then put a picture of yourself crossing the finish line from one of the races you have done along the way in a visible place. It will be a subtle reminder of where you want to go and it will help to keep that fire burning. You may find your motivation in a song or a movie. If you really want to get fired up, watch *Rocky* and listen to the pulse of "Gonna Fly Now." If that doesn't work for you, watch *Rocky II*, and if that doesn't work, try *Rocky III* and so on, and so on. In the final chapter, *Rocky Balboa*, there is a scene where Rocky is telling Pauley that he still has some fire down below and that is his motivation to enter the ring again.

It is all a matter of keeping the fire burning. If reading is your passion, then there are plenty of motivational books to help you keep your fire burning. Find an author whose work speaks to you and see where that takes you. The other day, I was watching the PGA Open, and one of the commentators was speaking about one of the players. What he said really struck me. The player was in a slump and the comment was simple and topical: "Just focus on the golf and the score will take care of itself." No matter your goal, it will be the effort that you put in that will get you there.

Focus on your efforts, and the goal will take care of itself.

The Millennial Challenge

The biggest challenge the Millennials may have is the need for instant gratification, recognition, and career advancement. This reminds me of the comedian Billy Connolly:

> ... We want this! And that. We demand a share in that, and most of that, some of this and fucking all of that. Less of that, more of this and fucking plenty of this. And another thing we want it now. I want it yesterday and I want fucking more tomorrow. And the demands will all be checked then so fucking stay awake.[2]

This generation may, at times, have to come to terms with the fact that getting what you wish for may only set you up for future failure. This is somewhat akin to the notion of the "one-hit wonder" in the music industry. You may rise to the top very quickly but that rise will not be sustainable in the long run.

True success is built on experience, and you need to take the time to gain that experience, particularly in the policing world where your decisions may impact the lives of others. At the other extreme, it drove me crazy when I saw people who were extremely talented, but had no motivation to challenge themselves. I saw that as an inability to deal with fear of the unknown and a lack of self-confidence, but upon reflection, it could be that they were just truly happy doing what they were doing. No matter how many years of service you have or what accolades you have received, you can always choose to go back to uniform.

---

2   Funny Comedian Quotes. Accessed at http://funnycomedianquotes.com/funny-billy-connolly-jokes-and-quotes.html?p=3

I did it a number of times in my service, and it was always good to go back to my roots. Going back still provides an opportunity for growth and chances are that, when you take on the next challenge, it will be easier for you to reach higher than you have before. It also helps you to develop more relationships and keep current with the frontline.

The Power of Positive Thinking

Motivation is a funny thing. It will mean different things to different people – what is critical is your *attitude*. It has to be positive, 150% of the time. When people ask you how you are doing, the answer should always be the same: "I'm doing great!" I guess you *could* tell them the truth when you are having a really bad day. I have done that a couple of times, just to get the response. Always look and act positive on the outside no matter what is going on. It is just like the picture of a duck on top of the water looking very calm, while seeming to glide effortlessly. If you look beneath the surface of the water, that poor duck is paddling to beat the band. This is in the context of your day to day work. Keep in mind, I am not talking about those times when you should be seeking assistance in dealing with some trauma you have witnessed from one source or another.

It comes down to the power of positive thinking, and you therefore want to surround yourself with people who are positive by nature. In doing so, you are continually giving yourself a kick in the ass, not to mention the people working alongside you. Remember you're on a journey, taking each step and each day, one at a time. The road will never be exactly the same for everyone. Some will take the shortest route, while others will take the most unorthodox detours, but in the end, most will reach their destination. You will then hopefully realize that all those valleys you went through to get to that point, were actually blessings in disguise. Trust yourself, and do not be afraid to call on a friend, a loved one, a parent, or a mentor to help you remain true to yourself. When a door closes, there will always be another door opening up for you. If the door won't budge, then take a leap of faith and try the window! If you develop a never-say-die attitude, you will be better equipped to face those obstacles and overcome them so that you can move on towards achieving your goals.

Chapter Eight Sound Bites
- Mama told me there will be days like this
- People will always expect/want more
- Find the balance between sanity and meeting those expectations

Chapter Nine
LEADERSHIP

So we wander round this desert
And wind up following the wrong gods home
But the flock cries out for another ...
And one more starry-eyed messiah
Meets a violent farewell

"Learn to be Still"
—Eagles, 1994

All Great Leaders are Visionary

Great leaders have been studied for centuries, and there are countless books written about the best and the worst of them. One of my bosses, mentors, and a great leader, Kevin, was particularly partial to Churchill and he would share the odd quote during the workday, and whatever it was, it always seemed appropriate and delivered at the right moment. At one point or another, if we are all expected to step up to the plate and be a leader, it's important to understand what it means to be a leader. Take some time to think about the great leaders you have known, either in history or real life. What qualities did they demonstrate? By definition, a leader is a person who commands, guides, and inspires others.

The *command* portion seems quite easy to understand, especially in a para-military organization with a clearly defined rank structure. The person with the highest rank makes the call, and everyone is expected to fall into place. In principle, this sounds pretty easy, but in practice, it can pose significant challenges. "A person who guides" also seems easy enough to accomplish; you get to be an armchair quarterback and call the shots. You will have been there and done that and you can make a decision with your eyes closed. Again, it is not necessarily as easy as it appears. Finally, the most important part, the *inspiration*, will likely prove to be the greatest challenge. Situations are different, people are different, so you have to constantly come up with ways to motivate your people to go out there and get the job done. This challenge can be fun, and how you approach it is really up to your imagination. It rests on your ability to understand yourself and your limitations as a person as well as the people you're leading.

> **A leader has to be someone who exudes confidence, especially in times of challenge or crisis.**

Not surprisingly, you will have to work on all aspects of your leadership profile on a continual basis, not only for your own professional development, but also because the playing field is always changing. Always ask yourself, "What qualities should a person demonstrate in order to be an effective leader? How effectively am I at behaving like the leader I aspire to be?" From my perspective, a leader has to be someone who exudes confidence, especially in times of challenge or crisis. They need to be steadfast and flexible in their decision-making and assume responsibility in both a fair and ethical manner. They need to show sincerity and care about the people they're leading. It really helps if you've been in the trenches because this gives you a mountain of credibility and allows you to not only talk the talk, but also to show that you can *walk* the talk. More importantly, when a controversial issue arises, and they make the wrong decision, a good leader will own their mistake, step up to the plate, be accountable, and then make the effort to make things right.

All great leaders are visionaries. They have the ability to look ahead and set a course that will be positive for both their people and the organization. A good leader will continue to remind themselves of these qualities and make a conscious effort to demonstrate this in front of their people. This brings us to one of the most important qualities a leader should demonstrate: transparency.

To demonstrate all of these qualities, you really have to be comfortable with yourself as a person. Not everyone is going to agree with you, and if you take this personally, it can tend to eat you up inside, which benefits no one in the long run. I am not saying that you have to develop a thick skin and disregard all criticism. Instead, you need to develop your self-awareness and understand that, whichever direction you have decided to go, you must set a steady course and be confident in your decision until you are provided with evidence to the contrary.

A good leader also knows when to remove themselves from their position of authority. For some, this is difficult because they enjoy the position and the power that comes along with it, making it extremely difficult to let go. I remember the first time I met Vern White. I was in Yellowknife, in the early 1990s, and it was not long after the Giant Mine explosion. Vern was a corporal and worked in one of the settlements at the time. It did not take long for him to find a position working on the murder investigation task force. He continued to climb the ranks, receiving a commission. At one point, I picked up a Sunday *Province* and noticed that he was the Chief of Police of Ottawa. Vern is now one of our senators.

I paid attention to his career only because I wondered about what type of leader he would become. I found some insight in that newspaper article, discovering some sage advice for anyone aspiring to assume a key leadership role in any organization. When Vern became the Police Chief of Ottawa, he came prepared with a five-year plan for the organization. It was his goal to accomplish everything in his plan within that five years and then execute his exit strategy. This was regardless of how well the Police Board liked him or how happy the community was with the service that was being provided under his leadership. If he were to stay any longer, it would be to the detriment of the community he served. It was his personal belief that a police service needs new leadership every five years so that they have someone with a fresh set of eyes and new ideas for the benefit of the organization's future service delivery.

What was missing in the article was the recognition that, in order for you to parachute into the highest leadership role of an organization facing significant challenges, you have to be a visionary. Vern did say that he had a plan, but I would guess that this was an understatement. He had a vision of where he wanted to take this force, with an eye to making improvements that would outlast his tenure. The trick is to ensure that each and every person knows what your vision is and believe in it – you need to spend the time to create buy-in. This means that you have not only communicated the vision but that you have clearly articulated how the vision will benefit the organization and your people. If you want to become an effective leader, you must be able to chart a clear path for the future.

Situational Leadership

> **Each and every one of us is a leader, whether we like to believe it or not. This is especially true as it relates to law enforcement.**

The question then becomes "How do you develop your vision and when do you start?" The answer to the latter question is *immediately*. Each and every one of us is a leader, whether we like to believe it or not. This is especially true as it relates to law enforcement. You show up at a scene and, quite literally, the world can be falling apart. People see you arrive on scene in uniform, and it provides a sense of relief and conveys the message that everything is going to be all right. The expectation is that you will be taking that leadership role, and I would strongly suggest you strive to do so with all you have to give. This is what is known as *situational leadership,* and I have heard many great stories exemplifying this and have been to awards ceremonies where individuals have been recognized for great leadership arising out of tough circumstances.

I am sharing this with you so that you take the time to get to know your inner leader and allow that leader to come to the forefront. Share your goals with your supervisors, and get their support to facilitate the needed development. Where you start will depend on your degree of confidence and whether you have an innate ability to function as a leader. As a leader, you must recognize your employees' efforts and determine how best to develop them so that they can excel and move forward in their careers. Give them opportunities that will stretch and challenge them, keeping in mind that they will also be developing the people around them and, as a result, the organization as a whole will benefit in the long run.

For some leaders, it is difficult to let their high flyers fly. When I was working with people who were more able than me, I was able to acknowledge this and give them the opportunities to let that grow without becoming jealous or jaded. A good example of letting people start small is to allow them to run a briefing with an investigative team, or a watch, or both. I remember when Bob Paulson, who went on to become Commissioner, was asked to come to our Integrated Homicide Investigations Team (IHIT) to teach us how to give proper briefings. I listened intently to what he was saying regarding the structure and purpose of a briefing and immediately began to employ his advice.

What we are really talking about is effective communication. It is a great place to start because, in briefings, you are talking about strategies or goals that you want to accomplish within a certain period of time, but in essence, you are sharing your vision about where you want to see the investigation go, and part of your job is to share this information with your team so they can move forward towards that end. This is one of the reasons that when I went back to uniform; I was bound and determined that everyone was going to contribute meaningfully to briefings. The manner in which they were traditionally conducted was quite dry and almost clinical in nature, with no real sharing of ideas or information. The information board was read, and then the team would hit the street.

Get Everyone on the Same Page

For me, it was an opportunity to share information so that everyone was on the same page. I set the ground rules by asking everyone to come prepared to the briefing. Each individual was to share one of the three types of information: something to do with officer safety, case law, or something they learned from one of their investigations that would be of benefit to everyone. At first, this was difficult because most people felt uncomfortable talking in front of others. After all, it is form of public speaking and that has a tendency to make some people nervous. Once I got my watch comfortable with this approach and I was in an acting officer's role, I asked the other watches to fall into place. This was a little more challenging because I was dealing with middle managers who were a little resistant. You need to repeat yourself again and again and lead by example. There were a few times where I had a challenge coming up with something to bring to a briefing, but I always managed to find something. When you think about it, you are talking in front of your peers and colleagues and sharing what you think is important. This is what leaders do on a daily basis, perhaps on a seemingly grander scale, but the process is primarily the same. If you let your team share in safe environments like this, there will always be a few who will rise nicely to the occasion. These are the people that you want to latch on to and hook them up with every rocket that is flying by.

I had a chuckle when I shared with a colleague that I let one of my constables run the briefing. His response was that it was like letting the chickens rule the roost. This comment couldn't be farther from the truth. This was an opportunity for me to develop someone. I could watch and see how the person did and then give him some constructive feedback in order to develop his skills and level of confidence.

Years ago, if you were a recruit at Depot who didn't know how to swim, you certainly did by the end of basic training. They threw you in the pool and it was, literally, sink or swim. They had long poles, and when you got close to the edge, you were pushed away from it. You eventually learned how to swim. I have said it many times before that, in a perfect world, we would have all the required competencies, and leading would be a breeze, but the reality is that we don't, so we have to develop our future leaders just like we developed the recruits who couldn't swim.

Provide Support

If all I had was someone with no experience to fill a tough role, then I would *put* them in that role. The secret is not to let them fail completely by giving them the support they need along the way, so that they come out with just enough bumps and bruises to have learned something, and enough desire and confidence to try the job again. There have been a few times where I have heard about people who, after being in tough roles, saying they were never going to take on that challenge again. As you are growing as a leader, you will need to always remember that even the worst of experiences provides an opportunity to learn. Some of the best learnings come from failures, for they cause us to really reflect on what we have done in order to avoid making the same mistakes in the future.

Observe the leaders around you and your immediate supervisor(s) to get a sense of your environment. This is not necessarily a question of understanding your role, but more one of positioning yourself positively in order to take advantage of opportunities. I have often said that it was my job to make my supervisor look successful. This is true, no matter what the calibre of supervisor. You should always be motivated to do the best job you can possibly do. Just do the best you can, and don't expect anything in return. You must strive to be positive and selfless. If you stay on your path, you will get to where you want to be, and who knows, if your supervisor gets promoted, you may be left with a good shot for promotion yourself. If you take the same approach when you get promoted, start with the same strategy but know that the situation and players are different, requiring you to adapt. It is important to remember that getting promoted should not be the main driver. The focus should be on developing your leadership skills, and that can be done at any level in the organization. Leadership is not just about formal position. Some of the most influential leaders can demonstrate their skills without a position to back them.

Your Job Is to Get Everyone on Board

Once you have made the decision to become a leader, you need to be aware that you will have varying degrees of support, ranging from one hundred percent to those who simply want to see you fail. To begin with, these people can only be seen as minor distractions because, as a leader, your job is to get *everyone* on board. This is a challenge in a paramilitary organization because, as I have stated previously, there is an expectation that you will do what a higher rank instructs you to do. At one point in history, it was simply known as giving an "order". In all my years of service, I never received an order, and I only ever gave one.

Expect that people will question your decision-making, and do not take offence. Years ago, to question a decision meant you were bucking the system. When someone questions you, you need to take this as an opportunity to communicate and increase their understanding as to why the decision was made in order to get "buy-in". This is not an easy thing for some people, and it may take some practice. You may be questioned, but you also may hear some great ideas that could assist you in adjusting your strategy.

I used to lead a course that included several case studies to solidify understanding of one concept or another. The process was the same for each case study. Here is the scenario (challenge); now tell me what are you going to do with it. The case study was presented to the class after providing them with enough knowledge to work through the challenge. After throwing it out to the class, I would share what I did and the reasons why. It was amazing how many new ideas popped up, ideas that would have worked better or would have been easier than the ones I chose myself. The point here is that, if you loosen the reins in front of your people to get their feedback, you are much better positioned when the next tough decision comes along. This also helps you to build credibility with the people you are leading, and it will go a long way in gaining their commitment to follow you.

By engaging your people, they will start to see you as someone they can trust as well as someone who is willing to actively listen. When it comes to climbing that new mountain, it will be much easier to climb because your leadership style will have resulted in people who are willing to crawl on broken glass so that you can climb that mountain. If you are following this person, you will not question why you are climbing the mountain; you will have that trust in your leader that it is the right thing for both you and the organization. That leader will also explain their vision to give context as to why you are climbing that mountain.

Strategic Thinking and Change Leadership

I have spoken about competencies in another chapter, but in the case of leaders, you will want to look at what the organization values. Sometimes referred to as "organizational" competencies, they outline the behaviours expected of leaders.

While it may seem like common sense, it has been qualified and quantified for promotional purposes in the RCMP. When I mention that a leader must be a visionary, I am referring to the competencies of *strategic thinking* or *change leadership*. Strategic thinking is defined as the process of being able to look at what is in front of you, identify challenges you would see in the future, and develop solutions to those challenges today. Change leadership involves championing the change in the organization that reflects that leader's vision. These are both very important competencies to understand.

The question I always have is whether you can really teach either of the competencies. I'm sure we all have qualities, to varying degrees, that will speak to our level or ability in those competencies. If I were to ask you just to stop and look at the way you are doing business today and identify those practices that will not work tomorrow, could you? I would suggest *yes*, but what about the solution?

The biggest selling point in any change management initiative is to gain commitment by showing the benefits.

We are not trained to think this way. It is stimulus response. What if you trained yourself to think this way? Look at just one problem, and make it simple, and come up with a solution. While you are at it, think about how many individuals will be affected by this issue tomorrow if you do not do something about it today. The biggest selling point in any change management initiative is to gain commitment by showing the benefits. Once you have come up with the solution, you need to think about an implementation plan and the people you will need to support you in this plan. Give yourself a timeline for this, and try your best stick to it. Put your plan into place, and after a period of time, assess how well you are doing. This is exactly the process I took when I realized that the ability of the front-line officers to conduct investigations had significantly diminished.

I have had the luxury of working with the crème de la crème for several years, and I also saw junior people with a lot of talent rise to the top. They always had someone along the way to help them, and they developed a strong foundation in understanding police work. When I went back to uniform for my last two years, I saw that this structure was missing, and I came up with a basic investigators program designed to meet the future demands of the organization. Sadly, I never had the opportunity to see whether it was successful.

These are those "side of the desk" projects, and because they are over and above your daily tasks, you have to create a sense of urgency if you are to ever bring them to completion. No matter what mark you hit, you will experience success to varying degrees, but the benefits to you, as a leader, can be phenomenal. You will not only begin to develop yourself as a leader, but also as a person with a reputation of caring for people, one who works to make things better for both the people and the organization. You will also be able to bring what worked and what didn't work to the next challenge, and you may become known for establishing the best practice in this area. Hopefully, you will have brought it to the next level, and the challenge for the level will be someone else's, but it will be your efforts that will have made a difference. The calibre of the people you will meet along the way will be amazing. You will want those people as part of your team or, for that matter, as individuals you want to follow because of what they bring to the table.

As a leader, remaining motivated will also be a challenge, not only yours but also that of the people you are leading. It is such an important consideration that I have dedicated a whole chapter to motivation. Your level of motivation, and how you convey it, will have a direct impact on the motivation of your team. Know this – regardless of how bad a day you are having, from a motivational perspective, when you go to work, you go to work with your game face on.

If you can see that your team's morale is down, it is your job to immediately do something about it.

Police work is a serious business, and if you can see that your team's morale is down, it is your job to *immediately* do something about it. Recognize that you will still have to deal with your own level of motivation, but that can come later.

I don't know how many times I went back to my teams and asked for more, knowing that eventually there would be a breaking point. The best thing that you can do in this case is to acknowledge your team's efforts and find a way to give them a break. This may mean a different assignment for a short period of time, or leave, or a combination of both. How many times can you draw on people who are exhausted and still expect to get the same results? If you are a strong leader, they will keep giving it their all, but in times like this, you also have to be a manager. Yes, there is a distinction between a manager and a leader. A manager is expected to plan, organize, and coordinate, whereas a leader is expected to inspire and motivate.

This is one of the interesting things about putting people in positions of authority. It usually comes to pass as the result of a promotion, whereby an individual has proven themselves at a lower rank level, and it is based on the age-old belief that past behaviour is the best indicator of future behaviour. Is their new role meant to be that of a manager, or that of a leader? This is not always clear, and you can get to the next level by demonstrating either set of competencies. I believe that what organizations are looking for are firstly good leaders, with the hope that they will become great leaders from there.

Hone Management and Leadership Skills

When you think about the ability to manage, you do not need to have rank to be good at this. It is just common sense and making sure that you have enough resources to get the job done over and over again. It is managing what you are doing with less. I think someone called that risk management. Thinking back to my position as watch commander, there were expectations with respect to numbers. I hate to use the word *quota* because it was not about quotas. This was a statistics-driven system, and the premise was that, if you did "x" number of *something*, the end result would be crime reduction. I would often say that I did not have to tell my watch what the expectations were, they always came from above. I had no decisions to make.

Long story short, the only thing left for me to do as a watch commander was to be a leader. As a leader, you learn how to move your team through both the good times and the bad, keeping your focus on the good times and the wins, both at the individual and team levels. It will not take you long to learn how to manage if you are so inclined. What you need to focus on is your development as a leader. If you hone both your management and leadership skills, you will know how to set the tone for your team in order to achieve better results and people who feel that they are making a viable contribution to the organization.

A great leader is one who is ethical to the core. When you are trying to decide between A or B, you should always ask yourself "What is the *right* thing to do?" This is always a good place to start if you want to be true to your values system. What is right can vary, depending on the situation, and there will always be a balance between your personal values and those of the organization. If you are looking for a strong investigator because you need that talent on your team, you will hopefully to be able to select someone from within your team. If you have done your job properly, then there should be more than one person in the running. No matter whom you choose, you need to choose the person that will bring the most to the team. What if there is a better skilled person out there who will not only fit the role, but who will also help the development of the team as a whole? If you have a great number of people on your team who are well qualified to do the job, and you do not pick one of them, what impact will your decision have on morale?

What is the right thing to do? What would you do? Take some time and think about this. What other factors do you need to consider, other than the obvious? In the end, it may be six of one and half a dozen of the other because, although the outside choice might be the best choice for the short term, what about in the long run? You could have a diamond in the rough on your team and not even know it. If you are committed to your team, and you have made it clear that you care about their development, the right decision may be to select one of your team members and, like any other time, set them up for success. If the skill set of the team is below what is needed, picking the outside choice is the right choice for everyone involved.

Know that when you finally make your decision, there will always be consequences. As a leader, people are always watching you. You are up on this pedestal, and some will want you to fail, some will want you to succeed, and some just will not care. You need to know and accept this because it may or may not get easier to deal with as time goes on. Where the lines start to get blurred is when it comes to organizational politics. The higher the impact of your decision-making, the more politics become a consideration. At the highest level in the

Force, it will be a balance of what is the best for the organization, its people, and the country as a whole.

The right thing to do might be the right thing for the country, but not necessarily for the organization, or its people. Such was the case when the Government of Canada clawed back some money from the Force's pension fund. It was all part of the government's deficit reduction plan. In the end, our

Remember. There will always be consequences, and sometimes damage control will be required.

contributions were increased in order to get the fund back to where it needed to be. It was great for the country, but it did absolutely nothing for the morale of the RCMP or that of its members. What was the right thing to do? Remember, there will always be consequences, and sometimes damage control will be required. A good leader knows this and is prepared to deal with this for the good of the organization and its people.

The consequences of your decision may result in lowered morale, and you will have to work to turn this around. The biggest consequence to you will be your reputation as a leader. The action that you take will largely depend on what kind of leader or reputation you want to have. Do you want to be seen as autocratic, or someone who is fair and the kind of leader that people want to follow? I would suggest that you strive to be the latter. In simple terms, think of you alone on an island. This island may be a tropical paradise or a desert island. It matters not because the island's climate will change over time. Learn how to get people to your island and you have become a leader.

Chapter Nine Sound Bites
- Find the leader in you
- Trust the leader in you
- Let the leader in you grow

Chapter Ten
THE SKY IS THE LIMIT

Hold your fire
Keep it burning bright
Hold the flame 'til the dream ignites
A spirit with a vision is a dream
With a mission...

"Mission"
—Rush, 1989

Legacy is the ability to make your visions(s) a reality. Great leaders have this ability, which really boils down to trust and self-confidence in putting thoughts into action. We all have visions, and not necessarily the ones Stevie Nicks refers to in the song "Dreams." We need to learn how to listen to others and develop something that is actionable. Is it thinking outside of the box? This whole "in the box" and "outside of the box" thing is all about perception.

I am letting you know that I am going to be all over the map here. I have to be because I am talking about visionaries. A visionary cannot be tied down when they want to go from the vision stage to the action stage. A visionary understands that, in order for a vision to become concrete, there needs to be flexibility. It is like being a prophet. Visionaries are tied to those different people, different personalities, and different environments. We all have this ability in us. To say that it is innate or can be developed is a matter of putting boundaries.

What if you did not know any better, and you had this fantastic idea, and you ran with it and saw it become a reality? Then you did it again and again.

This is no different than losing that innocence that we had when we were kids. At one point, society steals it away from us, and it never returns. It is not exactly innocence we are talking about here, but rather a quality that becomes suppressed over time, namely imagination or creativity. When I was a kid, I would wander off to play, and at times, I found myself staring up at the sky. It didn't matter to me whether it was a hot summer day or the dead of winter, I just needed to be able to see the clouds. I could make those clouds into anything. It was my own picture show, driven only by the confines of my vast imagination. It was imagination without borders, and literally, the sky was the limit. I can't remember the last time I did this, which is part of my point.

There are No Limits

Today's law enforcement leaders understand the need for visionaries

Somewhere along the way, we forget the importance of exercising our imagination. If you want to truly become the visionary you were meant to be, you need to reintroduce yourself to your imagination again and then let it loose. The accomplished visionaries have allowed this to happen, and it becomes a natural ability for them. For them, there still is "no limit" and you, as your own visionary, also have to believe there are no limits. Look at the people you know, and try and come up with examples of where they have allowed their true visionary to come out. It could be in art, it could be in sport, it could be in music, it could be in leading people.

I do not know how many times in the RCMP I heard one member say to another "*that* person has vision." At the time, all that did was create a bunch of questions in my mind that I was not smart enough to ask: "What exactly is a visionary, and how do I become one?" The individuals who can do this will likely have an impact on your career, simply by their example alone. This is not about success or failure; it is about getting to know yourself as a visionary and exercising your ability to push those limits. Think of it as having napped long past the time for waking up. If you listen hard enough, you will hear the alarm clock ringing. Do not hit the snooze button, jump out of bed and embrace your inner visionary like a kid on Christmas morning. Do not let anything or any person repress it, or push it back it back into slumber. Learn how to embrace it, and work to let it become a part of your persona.

It may sound kind of crazy to encourage police officers to develop the visionaries inside of them. The very nature of a paramilitary organization, bursting with structure and bureaucracy, naturally inhibits this type of behaviour. In spite of this, today's law enforcement leaders understand the need for visionaries and, in an attempt to solidify this, have identified it as a competency. In the case of the RCMP, it is called strategic thinking or strategic leadership, and it comes complete with a clear definition. What it translates to may be difficult to understand at first, but take the time to do so. It will be your gauge as to how much you have allowed your inner visionary to play a part in your law enforcement practice.

It can be defined as a process that dictates the manner in which people think about, assess, view, and create the future for themselves and others. In a practical sense, if you were not afraid to demonstrate this quality, you would always end up on the high end of the scale. Being on the high end of the scale, time and time again, will establish a reputation as a dreamer who is not afraid to try new things.

Build Your Visionary Law Enforcement Practice

The visions you come up with should seek to improve a work situation by raising the bar. It does not matter *which* situation, the steps that you will take will be similar. If you are a little apprehensive, start with yourself and become comfortable with the process. As your comfort level increases, you can let the scope of your vision expand as well. It is about coming up with an idea, creating a plan, and actioning that plan to make it a reality.

As it relates to the Force – or any organization– there are some aspects that are open to change, and there are others that cannot be touched. They cannot be touched because they are part of the traditions, the history, and part of the values that make the organization what it is. Not that long ago, I heard that a group wanted to change the words to "Oh Canada". The portion "True patriot love in all thy sons' command" was causing one group some angst. They wanted to see the word "sons" removed and the word "us" used instead as they felt it was more reflective of gender equality. I am all for equality, but I am not sure that I want to mess with our history. I personally feel that "Oh Canada", as Canada's national anthem, should be off limits with respect to a visionary's quest for change, regardless of the reason.

In the case of the Force, we do not want to mess with its rich history or change the values that have become intrinsic in its service delivery. Moreover, in this case, we want to encourage visionaries to develop their inner visionary so that the Force's rich history can sustain itself from one generation to the next, from one world to the next. We want those visionaries to take those values to the next level and see a better RCMP in the context of the same values.

Once you understand what is fair game, it is up to you to release your inner visionary, to learn how to master this process, and to get the most from your visions of grandeur. In order to accomplish this, you have to become self-aware and then tackle your surrounding environment. In learning to know yourself, really understand the way you think, the way *you* problem solve, and how *you* interact with others.

As an example, I read a book a few years back entitled *The Practical Dreamer's Handbook: Finding the Time, Money, and Energy to Live the Life You Want to Live*. It sounds like a bit of like an oxymoron because, being practical, implies limits that a dreamer should never have. One day, I was reading the book on the patio outside my apartment complex, and a person walked by and made a comment about this fact. I chose this book subconsciously, based on the way I think, my ability to dream, or how I thought I should dream. My point here is that you need to understand what will help your visionary qualities to grow, and this starts with introspection and being comfortable in your own skin. Along the way, you will also rely on your mentors.

A true visionary has a habit of walking down an unbeaten path, or navigating through uncharted territory. A true visionary is not afraid to hit a wall; they see it as an opportunity to try something different, understanding that obstacles are simply a part of seeing your dream become a reality. They understand that "a swing and a miss" is just part of the process of hitting a home run. The challenge is being patient in those times when you are feeling like there have been too many misses. Just consider it practice for the next time you're up to bat. Every now and again the Police Gods will smile on you, and your vision will become a reality.

Being a visionary is part of your law enforcement practice and needs to be embraced in your developmental plans. I know what you are thinking. How do I capture this in my plan? These plans always boil down to one or two sentences, and it will be no different here. On your part, it involves the realization that a particular issue, if not addressed, will negatively impact the organization down the road. It could also be an initiative that will assist the organization in going to the next level, whether it is from a skill set level, a relationship level, or an esprit de corps level.

In the context of a relationship, think about the integration in the Greater Vancouver area. With all the different police jurisdictions and police forces, there had to be an effective way of providing service that was built on stronger communication and the ability to work well together during investigations that spanned those jurisdictions. Years ago, this was a new concept, and the visionaries saw the need to move towards an integrated model for a number of different reasons. At first, the motives were reactionary, but today they are proactive as well. The visionaries chose a path that not only addressed the problems of that time but with a sight to tomorrow as well. I am not sure if this was by chance or design back then, but today it has to be by design.

The great thing about approaching service delivery from a visionary perspective is that it gives you drive, gives you motivation, and for those individuals who are not practical dreamers, the ability to go somewhere without really knowing where they are. The less practical dreamers find comfort in the unknown and are more effective with this mindset.

Live It and Breathe It

Law enforcement visionaries will take the time to coach others on how to be visionaries. As a leader, you need to ensure that this happens in a formal manner on a quarterly basis and, more informally, on a daily basis. This means that you need to live it and breathe it. You will be continually encouraging an environment that allows for this kind of thought and creativity. In the past, you could put your idea in a suggestion box. These boxes were usually small wooden boxes with those little suitcase locks on them. You did not have to put your name on it; you just put the idea in the box. That was followed by a phase where you could receive monetary rewards for having a great idea. We have come a long way since then, and I would suggest that it is because someone had a vision.

I had been at BCLC (British Columbia Lottery Corporation) for three months, and I was really learning to walk all over again. My supervisor met with me and asked me if there was anything that we could be doing better. This was a loaded question that needed some clarification. Should I answer this question as it relates to the efficiency of the job that is being done, or should I answer it from a visionary's perspective? With either approach, the sky was the limit with the answer. I did not answer the question right away. I asked him to let me think about this. As the conversation progressed, I was asked to take on a task that would assist in our service delivery. With the task being presented, and the important question still unanswered, I began to ask my supervisor questions in order to give me an indication of how far he wanted me to take this task or initiative. From my perspective, the most important question I asked was what *his* vision was with respect to this initiative. To gain clarity, I asked for both his short-term and long-term visions.

These are the type of questions our leaders need to answer when they are asked by the people they lead. It gives tone and structure to your leadership. Not only are we on the same ship, we all need to know where the ship is going. In this instance, my supervisor shared both of his visions with me. After hearing his response, I told him that I would draft something up that would address the task at hand, not to mention the things that needed improvement. When addressing how to do things better, we can also be talking about efficiency.

There are some great strategic managers that could answer questions like that without batting an eye.

Being a strategic leader is not the same as being a strategic manager. This is something altogether different. A strategic manager is an effective leader in the context of meeting deadlines and using resources effectively. From an organizational perspective, visionaries must enable these individuals in order to see their dreams come to fruition.

It is always helpful to look at history when we are talking about trying something new. Visionaries have been around since the beginning of time. Like most things, we often do not see the forest for the trees. How were some so lucky to develop themselves as visionaries? There is no answer; I do not know why fortune smiles on some, while others cannot seem to get a break. Who are some of the visionaries who have really given us a better world to live in? The first person who comes to my mind is Albert Einstein, followed by Benjamin Franklin, and finally, Leonardo Da Vinci. What I have found fascinating about the latter two is the number of inventions that can be attributed to them. Did you know Franklin invented bifocals and Da Vinci the machine gun? For some visionaries, it is almost like free association. Long story short, being a visionary is not a new concept, and it is not something only destined for the rich and famous.

Resistance is Natural

For those people who truly want to let their visionary come out, they may encounter some resistance. This is a natural response to new ideas or change and you will need to deal with this. I have already shared the monkey story with you, but what if I were to change the monkey story so that, at the end of the day, the monkeys are not pulling you down, but are tossing you into the air to reach higher levels? While you are up there, you throw a rope down to the rest of the monkeys so that they can join you. If you work in an office where the monkeys would rather throw banana peels in the air instead of tossing you up to the next level, you cannot let that bring you down to their level. When the monkeys are getting you down, you need to find a cheerleader. At some point, those monkeys will slip on those banana peels, and they will take a hard tumble.

Have you ever been in one of those meetings where a person is just bursting with enthusiasm with ideas and begins to share their vision? Some of the responses I have observed have been somewhat less than impressive. I have seen people roll their eyes and even come out and say that what was being presented was a stupid idea. To give the people who reacted in this manner the benefit of the doubt, I will put that down to insecurity, a fear of change, or possibly both. No matter how harebrained the idea may seem, never shoot the messenger. The idea may not be complete, but that is exactly what you want. You can really exercise your visionary imagination, and that will make the difference with respect to positive changes. Remember, tomorrow you will be that messenger.

No matter how harebrained the idea may seem, never shoot the messenger.

I was going to use the word 'may' in the previous sentence, but you need to discover the visionary inside you, and if I were your supervisor, that would be my *expectation*. It may seem uncomfortable at first, but it will become second nature in no time flat. Think of those professions that have to do this on a daily basis. It is alive in the advertising world where you need to come up with that catchy slogan that is going to knock the public's socks off. TV shows are very similar. *Saturday Night Live* has been on the air for decades now, but the format has not changed. Each and every week, they have to come up with new and exciting shows that will make their audiences laugh. The writers of the show are given this task and, by extension, they are forced to be visionaries every day. Perhaps "forced" is too strong a word because, when you have found your calling, then you have found your happy place. My guess is that the SNL writers are definitely in their happy place.

There will always be external factors that may get in the way of your dream coming true. Many these are based on financial considerations. If I had two great ideas that would have a similar positive impact, but I only had the money for one, when it was all said and done, would the second idea fall by the wayside, or would it come to fruition? A true visionary would see the organizational value in both and would strive to find a way to both ideas materialize. It may simply be a matter of a staged implementation. There is always tomorrow, which leads to my next point, time.

It's All in the Timing

Timing is everything in life. Sometimes we know that the clock is ticking and realize that our opportunity will soon be lost, and there are other times we are not even remotely aware of the timeline and end up missing an opportunity. How many times have you heard someone say, "It was an idea before its time," –or– "I have had that idea for years."? You need to be aware of the external factors, and if one or the other has created walls during your journey, know how to get around them or change it so that you can achieve your desired results.

Never become a one-hit wonder. Always stay humble when you hit that home run and know that you will only be as good as the last vision that you made a reality. Take credit where credit is due, and move on to the next challenge. You need to understand what success means as a visionary. It could start by going down some road and ending up in a completely different city or province. Would it matter if you were the one who navigated the trip if, when all was said and done, you met the goals you had set but in a totally different way than you anticipated?

As I have mentioned before, I had no desire to become a subject matter expert in legal applications, but the doors it opened, and the influence I had to make some positive changes for the organization, were fantastic, and it really does not get any better than that. I was constantly trying to come up with better ways of doing one thing or another. Although I had more freedom than most working in the unit, know that we all have freedom. It simply comes down to a choice. The choice is whether you want to be in sync with your potential and make the difference that you really want to make in law enforcement. This is not an easy thing to do as an individual, let alone as a unit, a detachment, or from an organizational perspective. It takes time and effort to invest in this type of thinking, but think of the inertia that will come along with this. It will be perpetual.

Visions are really opportunities for us, and they present opportunities to develop ourselves and others. In some cases, the opportunity is short lived, so never be afraid to seize the moment. If you fail to do so, it will likely end in regret. Yet, even with regret, there is opportunity to grow and develop. In the early 1990s, I was in Puerto Vallarta, and I went into the hotel store to pick up something. There was this guy right beside me, and I could not figure out where I knew him from. He was buying cigars. It then dawned on me that it was Tommy Lee Jones. I thought to myself that it couldn't possibly be, but then he pulled out his American Express card. In our business, we call this a clue. The card read Tommy Lee Jones. What did I do? Absolutely nothing. What did I want to do? Strike up a conversation, ask for a photo op and get his autograph. It was a lost opportunity. It was a great lesson for me to learn.

Fast forward a few years and there I am, seeing Gwen Stefani's tour bus parked outside of the hotel I was staying at in Berkley, California. I was not going to let this opportunity go. I saw the bus, and I began to walk up to it, and Bob, whom I was working with at the time, asked me what I was doing. I told him that I was going to talk to Gwen. I banged on the bus door and it swung open. There was this big, big guy with a lot of bling on him. Was I scared? Oh yeah. Being the consummate professional, I asked if Gwen was in. In his burly voice, he responded that she was not there. Well that was it for me; it was time for me to go. The size of that guy, coupled with the nature of his disposition, spelled potential trouble that was my second clue, and I knew that it was

A swing and a miss are better than no swing at all.

time for me to make my exit. Yes, it was a swing and a miss, but how many people do you know who can say that they banged on the door of Gwen Stefani's tour bus?

Look at fulfilling your dreams the same way. A swing and a miss are better than no swing at all. If people laugh at you when you tell them your dreams, ask yourself, "Why are they laughing?" They are probably laughing because they too have dreams but are too afraid to voice them out of fear of failure or fear of being pulled down by those monkeys.

Along the way, you will find people who are looking for their inner visionary. You will find people who have found it and are trying desperately to develop it. And you will find people who have totally embraced it. Find your inner visionary and become a champion. There is more than enough room for another visionary in the room. That room will never be too small.

Chapter Ten Sound Bites
- It always starts with a dream
- The only fear a dream creates is the fear of success
- Become a Champion of Dreams

Chapter Eleven
POLICING AT THE SPEED OF LIGHT

Pleased to meet you
Hope you guessed my name, oh yeah
(Who who)
But what's puzzling you
Is the nature of my game, oh yeah, get down, baby

"Sympathy for the Devil"
—The Rolling Stones, 1968

Digital Disruption

It was the early 90s, and I was policing in small-town Alberta when our detachment received a delivery. It was taken out of the packaging material and carefully assembled. It was placed on a desk as if the desk was an altar. I remember walking over to look at this gift from the gods. With reverence and curiosity, I wondered how this was going to help me throw bad guys in jail. That is when Gerry, the boss, came over and made the comment, "No one is to touch this, it is for the office staff only. I don't want you guys wasting your time on this." This made no sense to me, and not that I am a rebel, but I wasn't buying into this. This was cutting edge technology, and I was convinced this was a new tool for law enforcement. Cutting edge technology in the form of a stand-alone computer. It wasn't even networked, not that we knew what that meant back then. By today's standards, this computer should almost be in a museum.

On a very small scale this was my first real experience with "digital disruption" in policing. Digital disruption, like so many other concepts, comes from the business world and is the new wave in policing. It is the change that occurs in an environment when new technologies are introduced. It is funny when you think about disruption – it gives the connotation of something bad or even sinister. Perhaps that is why I chose the lyrics I did. After all, do we really know who we are communicating with on the internet at any given time? Like any change that is certain, it is how we accept it that will make the difference, and in policing, it is no different.

That stand-alone was just the tip of the iceberg. A few years later, I would have my own stand-alone, then my own cell phone, then my own laptop, and eventually my own BlackBerry so I would have information immediately and cold stay tapped into the network. Somewhere in between all of that our minds, interactions, lives were hooked into the internet, moving us closer to a Big Brother world.

Policing and Social Media

What followed was social media when Facebook popped its head up in the world. The police world responded with fear. We were directed to stay away from that for both security and safety reasons. Somehow that medium would expose us to some kind of threat and compromise our integrity. I guess this is no different to the line of thinking that you should never have your name and number listed in a phone book. It was a safety concern. Keep in mind that the tactic is to go to your friends and family's social media accounts as a means of getting to you. We now have LinkedIn, Instagram, Snapchat, Twitter and a host of other sites that are used for marketing and social networking. Every Police organization has its own website, its own Twitter handle, not to mention all the individual handles their officers have.

Truly, policing is now at the speed of light, and along with that, the public expectation that they immediately be informed of any new event through social media. Policing has come a long way in this sense, but it is, for the most part, uncharted territory. It needs to be embraced so that there is no question about the good, the bad, and the ugly of social media as it relates to policing.

On a personal level, and in the context of a civilian who has aspirations of a career in law enforcement, you have to be aware that any online activity is forever and will be the subject of any security clearance process. Wherever you go, you leave a digital footprint that will lead right back to you.

When I entered into my third career, I had to have a security clearance because I was working in a police environment. These applications are a pain in the neck because you have to list friends, associates, and family; you have to list the clubs and organizations that you belong to, and now because of digital disruption, your use of internet and social media is also investigated.

Remember Laremy Tunsil

So whatever you say or do that you upload to the internet will be scrutinized. To kick it up a notch, think about all the cameras that are constantly filming us while we wander around in public. Even these video clips end up on the internet and news feeds. To put this in perspective, think about Laremy Tunsil. If you do not recognize his name, this helps make my point. In 2016, Tunsil was destined to be the #1 pick in the NFL draft. Destiny had nothing to do with this. Tunsil, no doubt, put countless hours in on the football field and in the gym – and then it happened. His verified Twitter site was hacked, and before you knew it there was a video of him that had gone viral. It was a thirty-second video of him smoking drugs with a gas mask attached to a bong. His #1 position quickly slipped down the scale until he was drafted #13 by the Miami Dolphins. That thirty-second video cost Tunsil millions of dollars not to mention the impact on his reputation and career.

Like pro athletes, police officers are expected to be role models; the public expects a higher standard from those donning a uniform. Much in the same way as the scrutinize pro athletes, the media pays attention to what the police are doing on the beat. We have all seen the video of the officer appearing a little heavy handed while arresting someone. The source of the video, in most cases, is a cell phone. The video within seconds hits the internet and millions of people are watching a short snapshot of incident and making judgement on that without know what actions occurred prior to hitting 'record' and what actions occurred after the record button was hit again.

Welcome to the Age of Cell Phone Evidence

This is where my head was at when I was working a night shift in the Fraser Valley not just a night shift – a *weekend* night shift. We all like to let loose on the weekend, and what follows from that are calls that will be for the most part fueled by liquor. Any time the police have a chance to nip a potential problem in the bud, it is just common sense police work. One of my officers was doing exactly this as he was checking a community hall where people were gearing up to throw a dance. I stopped in to monitor the situation and help where I could. The organizers were bringing in ice, beer, hard liquor – your usual fanfare for a barn burner. There was just one slight problem. There was no liquor permit, which means no dance and a bunch of unhappy people. When *that* bomb dropped, things began to get a little heated, and the situation needed to be defused right away. This is not a new scenario; it is a common thing that police have engaged in for years: shutting down parties and telling people to go home. What was different in this case was that as soon as the bomb was dropped, out came the cell phones and people were recording our every movement and every word. This was the most uncomfortable feeling. I had done the job for over twenty years and always acted in a fair and professional manner and began to almost second guess my actions and decision making. I was under a microscope, knowing that anytime my actions could be seen on the internet – and what was worse was the word "viral" popped into my mind. It all worked out in the end; the situation was settled, and the party goers found an alternative solution to have fun that evening.

There is nothing *wrong* with this because the police will always be (and should always be) accountable for their actions and what better way to make them accountable than have their actions digitally recorded. Having said that, it is better when the police are doing the recording. It leaves little doubt with respect to editing. There have been several instances caught on video where the police appear to have conducted themselves well outside of public expectations. I always like to believe that these incidents are more the exception than the rule. The trouble is that the exceptions are normally put in the forefront and cause damage to reputation.

In my mind, it was more than reputation. When you have a police force that is giving their heart and soul to the public, and there a couple of bad apples that turn that south, it is not right. In fact, it is more than that – it is far from fair to those officers that have sacrificed themselves for what they believe in. The only way you can survive a blow like this is to not only give exemplary service, but to give that and then some. That is easier said than done. This is even more of a challenge if you are the chief of these officers. Social media can cast a dark cloud over the best of police organizations.

Social Media and Sharing Best Practices

Enough of the dark talk. I am one hundred percent an optimist. Having said that I am one hundred percent a realist. What this means is how can the police use this disruption to their advantage and make an even safer community? This can be done from several fronts. So how can the police use social media to enhance service delivery? It is a great medium for networking. Parents who have kids that play video games online can appreciate the power of this. When my son can play a video game with someone who is half way around the world, we can certainly share best practices in policing in the same manner. Just think about this for a second – and a second is all it takes. If I can contact a colleague around the world, and we share an idea that will make our communities safer, that is a win-win. I guess the best example we have of this is the Crime Stoppers program. It went viral in the 80s before we knew what viral was. The best we could have done with a real-time crime drama was in 1994 when the infamous OJ Simpson was being chased in Los Angeles by the police in his white Bronco. He would later be arrested for the murder of his wife, Nicole Simpson, and her friend, Ronald Goldman. Now this is conceivably a daily occurrence thanks to social media.

Most people have a LinkedIn account whether they know how to use it effectively or not. This is the whole point behind this website... to *encourage* people to network. Networking is one of the best activities to invest your time in. The same old adage, it is who you know. In the context of today's digital revolution it would be more a question of how you know them. There is a difference between having someone follow you on Twitter and having a lunch with them every second Thursday of the month. It does open the door, however, for a working relationship. I am still amazed by the amount of activity you can see on a Twitter feed. This site only allows 280 (originally 140) characters to send out a message. It was designed this way because it was meant to be used for texting, which only allowed for that many characters. There are a lot of good things on Twitter that can help you to network or point you in the right direction on one topic or another. It can be used as a 'how to' either from a do-it-yourself perspective or motivational. I even have my own Twitter handle @Mikechronicles. I throw out a daily tweet no different than a fisherman throws out a net. I never know what I am going to catch. I have four themes that I tailor my tweets to: #Leadership, #Work, #Life & #Music.

The Leadership tweets are aimed at those who are or want to become leaders and to get people thinking about the responsibility of leadership – those who want to become.

The Work tweets get people thinking about how to be successful at work.

The Life tweets are meant to get us to appreciate life a little every day and really think about what Life/Work Balance may look like.

#Music can best be described from a therapy perspective. Music means different things to different people. I choose songs from all genres, and the tweets are based on lyrics of a song or vice versa. In either case a message is there.

The great thing about these tweets is, at least *my* in mind, there is always someone on the cusp of making that first step to something positive in their life, and that tweet may be the words that put them over the edge and truly get to that place they want to go. They are created with no one and everyone in mind and are meant to be received with curiosity in the context of the individual who received them. This sounds a little hokey, but in the end, we all have to find that motivation or desire to kick our dreams into gear. If one person finds that in 280 characters, then it is all worthwhile.

Code of Conduct

Every police officer, regardless of force, will have a code of conduct they must follow. In British Columbia, you will find this in statute in the *Police Act*. The code speaks to the expectation of how the police show conduct themselves with specific ethics and values in mind. The code also has a list of actions that are referred to as "disciplinary defaults". This list includes neglect of duty, abuse of authority, and considering the point of discussion "Improper Off-Duty Conduct". Any activity on any website by an officer can be considered for a breach of this code and potential disciplinary action. The code is meant to be no different than any other aspect of police work and is based on common sense. It does have an added public shock test included with it. This is a good gauge anyone should have when deciding to hit the send button or post a selfie that borders on being inappropriate. If the public is not good enough for you, then just ask what would Grandma think. I would think that you will now find specific policy that governs the use of social media by our officers.

> **In keeping with the common sense aspect of using social media both on and off duty, for those have aspirations of becoming the next "Mr. or Ms. Big" in an undercover scenario you can kiss it goodbye if you have plastered yourself all over the internet and identified yourself as a police officer or associated to any police force.**

On an organizational level, social media can be of great value from a service delivery perspective. The first question I have is, "Do the police want to be reactive or proactive in the use of social media and service delivery?"

Like any good lawyer would respond, *it depends*. I would think a little of both, and I say this because of the speed at which information is shared across the net, which means that police, at times, may have no choice but to be reactive. In a perfect world, it should always be from a proactive position. This assumes you have endless resources in place to accommodate this type of service delivery. This is never practical.

The message has to be strong that policing has to get with the times and engage in social media to solve crime, fulfill community policing expectations, and keep the public informed almost on a real-time basis. In 2011, Vancouver became the victim of another Stanley Cup riot. It was Game 7 and the Boston Bruins were in town. I recall listening to the news broadcast about the information that came across social media prior to the *spark* of the riot. There were messages specifically encouraging people to go downtown to engage in the riot. It fueled the crowd-like mentality to cause the damage it did. As much as social media inadvertently gave the nameless crowd a cohesive front, it also became an effective tool for the Vancouver police to begin to piece things together after the fact. It would lead to the identity and support of prosecution of countless individuals, a sad thing for those individuals who got caught up in the crowd mentality. This line of thinking usually gives a sense of anonymity for those involved. Social media takes this element out of the equation.

There are police departments and officers that have learned how to use social media in their everyday practice. All we have to do is take a look at what the Delta Police Department is doing in the lower mainland of BC. Going to their website, you get a sense how social media has become a part of their law enforcement strategy. Looking a little further, you will see the use of Twitter having first a general Twitter handle, Unit handles, and a few officers that have their own Twitter handle. Cst. Sarah Swallow's handle is @CstSwallow, and when you go to her site and look at her tweets you will see how effectively she uses Twitter to communicate with the public. Her tweets contain information about recruiting, traffic, accidents, and even the Delta PD's Community report. Simply, these reports let the public know where the challenges are in policing and how the department plans to address them.

Real Time Intelligence

Now we have "Real Time Intelligence Centres" designed to assist investigations by giving real time clues to assist with crime-solving ability. These centres have the ability to access information from an everywhere perspective which will include social media. With an abundance of information, the police are adept to identifying key information to advance investigations. This is commonly referred to as data mining. I could not have imagined using this term when I began policing.

One of the biggest challenges the police have in Canada is that it relies on a *Criminal Code* that has not embraced technology. An example of this: in 1974 laws were enacted to allow the police to intercept private communications to solve crime. This when people communicated with land-based telephones yet today those same laws are used to intercept private communications through cell phones, the internet, including social media sites.

Even more complicated is the fact that these communications can take place anywhere in the world, bringing a whole new complication to the party – extra-territorial jurisdiction. The police in Canada can only police in Canada, so if their suspect or witnesses are behind a computer half way around the world, how does this work? The public, in an instant, become judge, jury and executioners seeing the crime unfold in front of them in real time.

Social media and the internet are nothing to be feared. As soon as something becomes feared because a lack of understanding, it controls us. You need to know what it is capable of doing for you and what the boundaries are from a number of different fronts. Know

Know that there is no separation from personal use of social media and use as a police officer. The two are still related to you.

that there is no separation from personal use of social media and use as a police officer. The two are still related to you. It is really more a question of how you want to tame this beast and continue to use it for enhanced service delivery. This does not mean – and *cannot* mean – that whatever we learned over generations of policing is placed aside to create a new model. Remember what I said about Drive-thru Policing. Relationships will always be key. Missing this point is like listening to the song only for the music without really paying attention to what the lyrics mean.

Chapter Eleven Sound Bites

- The internet is forever
- What changed a second ago, will change a second from now
- Digital disruption causes a wave; learn to wave back

Chapter Twelve
FOOLS AND SAGES

Half my life's in books' written pages
Live and learn from fools and from sages
You know it's true
All the things you do, come back to you

"Dream on"
—Aerosmith, 1973

Two of My Sages

It was early evening, dark. The weather was damp. Typical fall weather in the Lower Mainland, and I was working yet another homicide. This one was different, though, for the stakes were higher, and we were after a serial killer. After surveilling our target, it was time for a break, and I needed to make a phone call. I had no idea how this phone call would impact my life. I just wanted to find a place to rent while our house was being built. I got off the phone and said to my partner: "I can't believe this guy, I only want to find a place to rent, and he says he wants to be a friend." As a cop, you initially think that everyone is lying and you do not easily trust. You do this in order to survive, and now, out of the blue, a perfect stranger wanted to be my friend.

I met Magdy at his house to see the suite and left feeling like I had gone through a job interview. My options were limited, so we moved in. During that first meeting, Magdy professed to be an Olympian, a ski instructor, a psychologist, and an aviation engineer. I called "bullshit" and then did a little research on this mystery man. I found evidence that he had fenced in the 1968 Games in Munich, but I was still skeptical. Then again, if his claims were true, I knew that I could learn something from him.

This is the interesting thing about sages, they will present themselves at various times in our lives, and it is up to us to take notice or not. We were not meant to walk on this planet alone, and you are fooling yourself if you believe differently. To be successful, you have to be willing to check your ego at the door and expose yourself to someone, exposing all your cracks and insecurities. It is the ultimate giving of trust, but by understanding our weaknesses, we become stronger. You are sharing what is most personal to you in the hopes that they will give you that magical advice that will steady your course to success and happiness.

It is hard to know when to take that leap of faith and trust in someone, but there is only one way – by slipping over the edge. If your leap pays off, then you will have made a connection, and a door opens. A connection gives you the confidence to take this chance and share what you want to do with your life and where you want your career to go. I slipped over the edge and began to put my trust in Magdy. Over time, I became comfortable and shared my thoughts with him. He was always willing to share his unique perspective on the situation. Magdy was a mystic. The ironic thing about that is, as much as you are looking for the answers from these masters, mystics and gurus, they are people who want to connect with you as well. They want sage advice from *you* and may include you in their deliberations of a decision involving a relationship or a financial or career choice. Never think that you have all the answers, but be willing to share what you know.

Dad was my hero, my friend, and my most important and trusted confidant. He joined the RCMP in 1957, at the age of nineteen and was loyal to the Force and a devoted family man. No matter what the problem or challenge, he had the uncanny ability to sit there and listen. His manner made you feel comfortable, regardless of how serious the trouble was, and it was easy to confide in him. He was the ultimate master.

There was another thing that he would share with me that would impact my life for years to come. He had another family, a family that would become mine:

the RCMP. At that time (and I would say even today) you would do anything for another member to help them. There was no Seinfeld banter about when it was time to help somebody move. If they were a member, you just did it. Being a member of the RCMP family made it easier to find masters, mystics and gurus. It was this family connection that made it easy to make sage connections. There was a common bond, and the RCMP family cared about you, your family, and your career.

Dad had great people skills, and it did not take much for him to strike up a conversation with a perfect stranger. Having witnessed this many times, it would not take long to hear him fire up a laugh. He was even-keeled and kept his emotions in check. Remember, you had to be as tough as nails back then, and just deal with your emotions anyway that you could. I can count on one hand the times I saw him get angry.

When I look back, it was not surprising what happened during a visit when I was five years old. I was asked the question that adults love to ask kids that age: "What do you want to be when you grow up?" Not having a care in the world, I immediately blurted out what was on my mind: "An RCMP." All I remember hearing was laughter. That was the day my destiny was set in stone and Dad became my guide, helping me make it to the beginning of that journey, and beyond. I thought that my dad knew everything and could do everything.

I learned a valuable lesson from him when I was in my early teens. Mom was a devout Girl Guide leader and would go to one of their camps just outside of Ottawa, Camp Woolsey. Dad volunteered to do some handyman work at the camp. I went along, not only to be with Dad, but also to help with the task at hand. He was installing a hanging ceiling and began working without hesitation, and soon the ceiling was starting to take shape. It was getting close to being done. There was nothing more precious than time alone with Dad.

We are always in awe of our heroes, and I asked him how he learned to install one of these ceilings and just about fell off my chair when he told me he had *never* learned and that this was the first time he had done this. I was in a bit of shock and did not know what to think. The master had taught me a

You can do anything you want to if you put your mind to it.

valuable lesson that day: I learned that my dad was not perfect and that he did *not* know everything. This could have been looked at as a chink in his armour, but really it was just something that made him stronger in my eyes.

More importantly, it is what this admission of my father's did for me. It taught me that you can do anything you want to if you put your mind to it. Furthermore, I began to understand that you have to put yourself in different and new environments, no matter how uncomfortable they may initially make you feel. This lesson helped me develop confidence to try new things, no matter what the task or the location. Developing confidence in your abilities and yourself is the key to personal success.

Police work is kind of a funny thing. It puts you in so many different environments and situations. On the front line, you have to be a jack of all trades. You need to know how to take statements, write warrants, book in prisoners, and attend community meetings – essentially whatever it takes to get the job done. In the old days, if you were asked to do something new, you would just grab a file from the file room and mirror whatever what had already been done in that file and the job was done. It certainly wasn't the best practice because it was based on the assumption that whoever had worked on the previous file did the right thing. It did give you some insight into proper documentation and supporting paperwork, but there was nothing that could prepare you for the things that happened on the front line. There, you could be attending a fatal motor vehicle accident, or arresting a dangerous person by taking then down at gunpoint. In these situations, experience is the only way by which you will gain confidence. The important thing was that you always relied on your training and common sense to come out of those situations unscathed.

I know that the one thing that even Dad did not teach me was to know my limitations. I would have to rely on another sage to teach me about limitations. Early on in my career, I would share these stories with Dad. I just assumed he could relate as a policeman, but it was not the case, he could relate more as a father. Being a member in Ontario was nowhere near the same as serving in what we referred to as a "contract" province. In the contract provinces, the members were real policemen, and they did everything that all of our municipal police officers would do. In Ontario, it was different; often the Members would be characterized as guarding tulips on Parliament Hill. This is why, at one point in time, in order to work in Ontario, you had to have at least five years of service in a contract province.

Growing up, I had no appreciation of this distinction, and it did not matter to me because Dad was still my hero. I did not have to seek his approval. He would always roll with the punches, no matter how difficult the issue was at the time. As I grew older and developed myself as a person, my relationship with him only got stronger. I could say the same for Greg, Chris and Anne, my other brothers and sister, and, later on, with their partners. We moved to the interior of BC when he retired from the Force, and he accepted a job managing a feed store. Shortly after that, I found myself with a part-time job in the store, and Dad became my boss. I think this took our relationship to a different level because, as my boss, I wanted to prove myself to him as a good employee.

Music and Life

When I started making a little money, I soon purchased my first car, and like most kids, I had a car stereo. I began to collect cassette tapes, and I remember one in particular, "Eagles Live", which was released in late 1980. It was a summer day, and I was cranking some tunes from this cassette and I heard Dad singing along to one of these songs.

Music was also something that shared in common and it was Eagles' "Long Road Out of Eden," released in late 2007, that would be the last music gift that I bought for Dad prior to his passing. He showed me the importance of understanding how music can impact your life from many different perspectives. It can provide motivation and act as therapy when you're going through rough times. I have often said that, if we were stop and think about this, we could all come up with a set list that we could call the soundtrack of our lives. Think about what your track would be.

You see, music brings people together, and it helps you to identify with others with whom you may not have otherwise connected. It does not matter what the genre, music is a great way of bonding with someone. If you are a country fan and find yourself with someone new, it is easy to strike up a conversation about the songs and artists that you like and/or despise. It does not matter whether that individual likes country or not because they will share that with you, and the conversation may evolve to discussions about other types of music.

When I first started listening to music, I really did not appreciate the lyrics, but later, I started listening to the words, and in some cases, I wondered about the underlying message. The funny thing about music is that it will mean different things to different people at different times in their lives. It has been a part of our lives almost since the beginning of humanity, and it will continue to impact our lives. Without knowing it, Dad imprinted something on me that has had a great impact in my life. I am sure that many people can relate to this.

It is not only music that makes it easy to strike up a conversation with a perfect stranger; there are a number of other topics that make it easy to have these conversations. As a police officer, you have to be able to make an instant bond with an individual so that you can bring some closure to whatever you're working on. It doesn't matter whether it's a noisy party complaint or a serious crime. The latter just means a string of individuals with whom you will have to develop rapport quickly. You can talk about the weather, sports, the stock market, or the real estate market. I just find that music is something that transcends generations.

If you want to learn more about dealing with people, I would suggest you read one of Dale Carnegie's books, *How to Win Friends and Influence People*. It was first published in 1936, and millions have been sold. Like music, the manner in which we develop relationships will never change, and Carnegie offers some great insights into this.

Dad's ability to get along with anyone and everyone showed me the importance of relationships, no matter how brief or transitory they may be. The reason he had the ability to get along with everyone was that he did not judge people. He treated them as he would want to be treated, with no consideration of their background, their skin colour, their gender, or their profession. This would be an important lesson that would affect my future relationships and how I interacted with people, while working as a police officer. When I say people, I mean the people I worked with, the general public, and the criminal element. You do not have to develop relationships with these people, but you do need to establish a rapport in order to get your job done.

One day, I had a junior member in my office, and we were talking about his development and his career path. During this conversation, I was quite surprised and puzzled when he revealed that he did not like dealing with street people. I told him that he did not have to invite these people to dinner, but that he needed to know how to interact with them in order to do his job. He was judging these people because of their lifestyle and involvement in crime. The same can be said of our colleagues. There are people with whom you will work and the relationship will only develop to the point that is needed to get the job done. If you develop a lifelong relationship with one of your colleagues, consider it a bonus.

Even to the end, the master was giving me sage advice, and how fitting the soundtrack was for this. Who would I go to now? My support system was no longer intact. Here is the danger, I knew what my support system was, but before I knew it, it disappeared before my eyes. He was my "go-to guy". When my world was falling apart, he was there for me, but no more. What was worse was the fact that I did not understand how to grieve, but I was smart enough to know that I should seek some help.

Build Strong Support Systems

It is at times like this that "gurus" often appear in our lives. They do not have to be psychologists or psychiatrists; they may be someone who has gone through that same experience and can help you find the way. I went and saw a psychologist over a period of time looking for answers on how I was going to carry on without my dad. I found solace, but there really isn't anything that will fill that void of losing a parent. It did allow me to appreciate what Dad's relationship meant to me and how he impacted my life. This guru helped me find a way to say goodbye.

For me, it was more a question of finding a symbol of Dad. A symbol that would allow him to be close to me and help to fill that void. It did not take long to come up with something because he loved eagles. These birds are characterized as being powerful and they soar through the sky with the highest level of confidence. It was time for me to get another tattoo, and that is what I decided to do. I would get a symbol of an eagle tattooed on my right calf. By this time, Mom was battling cancer, and I had a yellow rose put just below the eagle. The yellow rose meant something between Mom and Dad. He would always get her yellow roses for their anniversaries.

The fact of the matter is that Dad would always be a part of me, and he really gave me all I needed to know so that I could make it through this life. Still, you need that someone you can go to and bounce your ideas off.

The sessions with the psychologist were really helpful, and they helped me to eventually move on. Do not be afraid to reach out to professionals during difficult times in your life, it will only make you stronger as a person, and you will be better prepared when you find yourself in another difficult time. This reminds me of a time I was told a story about an officer I worked with/for, who found a guru while he was working a serious crime investigation. He had little time on the force and found himself dealing with a challenging investigation. A seasoned investigator gave him a helping hand, and he made it through this difficult time. This forged a relationship, but I also benefitted from this, as this guru would later come to work with us, and I also approached him for career advice.

> **Do not be afraid to reach out to professionals during difficult times in your life**

Magdy was not the first person I knew who immigrated to Canada and became successful. It always intrigued me how a person could land out of nowhere and, with determination and hard work, make something of themselves. This is not to say many Canadians have not accomplished this, but as Canadians, we have really become comfortable in our lifestyles, or in Magdy's words, "Fat Cats". We should never lose that "eye of the tiger" for fear of becoming a Fat Cat. One day, during our many talks, I asked Magdy about this and asked him what is up with Canadians. He would go into his rant about the system and how Canadians are afraid to succeed. How could that be? Canada is always world class, especially when it comes to hockey. It was more about how we, as Canadians, are made up. We are polite and have a great work ethic, but at times, we seem to be missing that certain characteristic.

I think what he was getting at was being professionally aggressive. In his mind, this would transcend from sports to business, and to one's personal life. You could tell that he had an edge, and my thought was that, if I could learn anything from him, I was all over that. Who else tells you to have "a very successful day" at the end of their voicemail message? I would come up to pay my rent, and we would have coffee or tea together. I remembered back to that initial phone call and realized I was starting to develop a relationship with Magdy. I would share with him what was going on in my family and he would reciprocate. We would talk about business and whatever else was going on in the world. We also talked about real estate investments, and he would give me pointers on that. I had no properties at that time, but what I *did* have was a whole lot of drive – and the need to make up for lost financial time.

As time would go on, Magdy would become an important part of my support system. This became even more important when Dad passed away. He did not replace Dad; he simply gave me support from a different perspective. No matter what he was telling me, he always left it up to me to make my own decision. It did not matter what the decision was, he always had a process. He told me on more than one occasion to have a plan, a backup plan, and then a backup plan for the backup plan.

> **Have a plan, a backup plan, and then a backup plan for the backup plan.**

I have used this line countless times when facilitating one of my many courses. There is seldom just one way of doing something, and there are a number of what some would refer to as the "Police Gods" at work. Every once in a while, you will come across a great witness or piece of evidence, and that is when all the preparation pays off. It is because of the preparation that you know exactly what to do when this falls into your lap. I guess another way of phrasing this is to expect failure. There is a corresponding disappointment that comes with failure, but I believe that, ten times out of ten, the failure creates a number of opportunities ripe for future successes.

Magdy was all about mental preparation, which was not surprising, considering that he was an Olympian, because that is more than half the game once you have prepared yourself physically. It was not beyond him to hone how I would look at a situation. As an example, he would ask me, "On a scale of ten, how much do you trust what I am saying?" No matter what the scale was in reference to, the answer was never ten, it was always higher. How can this be if the scale only goes to ten? In Magdy's eyes, if you picked ten, you were putting a limitation on yourself and you should never do this when earning your success. It also begs the question as to who is in control of your success. You are, and you always *should* be, no matter what the environment or who the people are.

Like any relationship, over a period of time, you are blessed with learning more and more about a person, which means both the good and the bad. At times, you even get to see someone's soft side. This is actually where you want to go, and in Magdy's case, this took some time. This gets back to the importance of building trust with people as you go through life. It was then that I felt confident enough to ask Magdy something personal. It would be personal for him, but it was more selfish on my part. Dad was already gone, and I had lots to remind me of him, but what if Magdy was to get his calling to a higher order, what would I have to remember him? I had been in his house several times and saw all his sports medals. They had to be symbols of success, as he proudly displayed them in his house. I finally got up the courage to ask him if he would give me something to remind me of him. I told him that I wanted it to be a reminder that I could keep and that it would be important to me. I told him to think about it and then to get back to me on it.

Not long after, I was up visiting Magdy, and he had picked out the item. What was the item that would remind me of what Magdy stood for, what he was all about, the item that would continue to provide that inspiration during the tough times after he was gone? He handed me a 3" x 3" fridge magnet with some writing on it. It said, "How old would you act if you did not know how old you were?" I accepted this token of friendship, but I was a little puzzled, to say the least. It was another test to make me think, a test that forced me to put life in perspective. You can take whatever you want out of this, but in my mind, it again speaks to limitations. You cannot put limits on yourself as you get older. You have to stay sharp, both physically and mentally, no matter your age.

I remember when I was trying to get myself back into shape and I was talking to Magdy trying to get some advice. It was plain, simple, and effective: "Don't stop." It was one step beyond NIKE's "Just do it". I wrote this on my whiteboard, but added a word to it: Don't stop, *ever*. Life will always be filled with peaks and valleys, but you have to be consistent with whatever you do in life. Let's not forget that it is a marathon, no matter whether the race is business, career, building wealth, or as in the case of Magdy, developing relationships with those people who will not only want to share with you how they met with success, but also share your successes as well.

There have been a number of people I have run into who have given me good sage advice that has helped me get a job done or tackle a problem in a certain way that guaranteed success at the end of the day. If you can find them and develop both personal and working relationships with them, you will have a friend for life.

In order to succeed, you need to get along with people, along with the gift to talk to people about anything and everything, without ever passing judgement. You need to treat people with respect. It does not matter who these people are. In policing, this means your colleagues, support staff, the janitor, the delivery people, the general public, and more importantly, the people you will investigate. You cannot be afraid to try something new nor can you be afraid to make mistakes. Without the mistakes, there can be no development. Remember what I said earlier about "Make it good". These are just some of the things Dad taught me. This is just the beginning because, in order to succeed, you have to mentally prepare, you have to be in control, and you have to be true to yourself as to where you want to go and how you want to get there. You have to be the ultimate professional and know that, when you limit yourself, you limit the chances of your success.

Through learning all of this, comes confidence. You will gain the confidence to deal with those times where you don't succeed at first but keep trying, and heightened confidence when you do succeed because, with success, come new challenges. These new challenges will test you at even higher levels, and you will experience different degrees of success. Know that you will need a support system to help you navigate your successes and always keep your eyes open. Sometimes you will look for these people, or life will just present them at the appropriate moment, at other times they will be a relative or a friend, but one thing is certain, when you realize who they are and the important role they play in your life, you will never let them go.

Chapter Twelve Sound Bites

- It is always 50/50 call a friend
- Sages are like angels, they show up in the strangest places
- You are tomorrow's sage

Chapter Thirteen
EVERYONE HAS A SOUNDTRACK

I wanna be that song ...

... When you're searching the horizon
When your eyes look back
When you're standing in the moment
Every life has a soundtrack

"I Wanna Be That Song"
—Brett Eldredge, 2016

It's always there, we just don't always notice it. You walk into a place or you're on a trip, and if you listen closely enough, you will hear it. Then it happens; you did not plan it, but it strikes you, and you are overcome with emotion. You have to stop what you are doing, and for a moment, you become lost. You find yourself in a place where you never expected to be. Sometimes it is a happy place, a sad place or, even a funny one. You have no choice but to follow because it was that song that came out of nowhere that took you there. This is what happens to me every time I hear "Wayward Son" by Kansas. This experience is intensified when you truly listen to the lyrics of a song and focus on the message it is imparting.

Early in life, Dad introduced me to country music. Every morning, the FM radio would be blasting everything from Johnny Cash to Loretta Lynn. What else could I expect from a Prairie farm boy? Today, some millennials may think of this as child abuse, but it did two things for me. First, it created a bond between Dad and me. Secondly, it gave me a real appreciation for music – an appreciation that continues to this day. Music is always changing, and as much as there are a multitude of genres, there will always be lyrics that will touch you, hold meaning for you, and help you through your life. Music will be that one element that stops you time and time again. It helps to shape and define a person, a group, a unit or a country. Just think about how you feel when you hear your national anthem being sung.

Music Evokes Memories

I think that a large number of us underestimate the importance of music in our lives. It has been around since the beginning of man. There is even a theory that while we were in the womb listening to Mom and Dad's favourite tunes, those melodies began to shape us and became part of our identity. Today, technology's ever increasing advances and the role that it plays in our lives has made musical access virtually unlimited. When I was a child, I remember watching Walt Disney every Sunday night, and it would always begin with the same musical theme. Tinkerbell would fly around Cinderella's castle as the magical music played, and then the show would begin. It was no wonder that when I visited Disney World for the first time, as an adult, I had goosebumps when I heard that music just prior to the park opening. For me, it is amazing to realize the power that music has over our subconscious.

There is little difference between music and police work. I have often made the comment about everyone having a personal soundtrack, and I would often ask others what theirs would be. A ridiculous real life example of this is a TV show from the 1990s called *Cop Rock*. There you were, watching this gritty police drama and then all of a sudden the whole cast would break into song. Subliminally, it reinforced the important role that music played in my life and the fact that, as I began to mature, I began paying closer attention to the lyrics.

With some songs, I conduct some research to determine what inspired the artist to write that particular song. For example, Don Henley's song "The Heart of the Matter" is about relationships ending while coming to grips and understanding that it is about forgiveness. If you were going through a divorce, or ending a relationship, this song may have help you find solace. The important message in the song is forgiveness, but the question is who needs the forgiveness and that will depend on the nature of the relationship. Do you forgive yourself for entering into that relationship or, as the song suggests, do you forgive the loved one who caused the pain? You have to really listen to the message before you can act upon it. I am not advocating that you have to put that record on the turntable and play it in reverse to hear the satanic messages telling you to do bad things. Just be curious about the lyrics and reflect on what they mean to you. They may mean nothing today, but years down the road, when life has offered you more experiences, perhaps the meaning will resonate with you.

When I was young, music was simply part of my social development. The first time I heard Bryan Adam's "Cuts Like a Knife," I was laying on the couch, and the music video came on TV. I was young and impressionable and, all these years later, can still see that music video in my head. The music sparked something in me. It was not until my later years that I could draw any meaning from the lyrics. I finally realized that the message is that with real love comes real pain. I have always seen this in a positive sense because it lets us know that, after feeling something that intense, we have to do something to change the situation. Most people who have gone through a failed relationship can relate to this. It is enough for you to say that you never want to feel that type of pain again. This does not mean that you should never love again because life without that kind of love can be quite empty.

Music can cause you to laugh, to cry, and to sometimes just feel warm all over. Sometimes it acts as a motivator, providing that little kick to get you exercising. The greatest thing about music is that it is up to us to choose the type or types of music that will do that for us. If you think about it from the flip side, maybe it is actually the music that is choosing us. Perhaps it is the music that decides what our soundtrack is going to be. In the end, whatever those melodies are, they will be a reflection of you.

Dad's Soundtrack

When Dad passed away, I remember collecting a bunch of pictures; you know the ones, all the ones that evoke great family memories that said *this is Dad*. The next thing I did was to create a soundtrack. It may have even been Dad's soundtrack, of this I am not certain. It is what I would have had as Dad's soundtrack, providing the means to spark all those memories of Dad. On the Eagles' latest album, there is a song sung by Glen Frey called "You are not Alone". The song starts off with the words, "Say goodbye to all your pain and sorrow ..." and is followed by "... Now you're standing in the light ..." For me, these words were a way for me to tell Dad that his pain was finally over and that he could go on to that place where you go when you leave this earth, perhaps a better place. On that same soundtrack, I included Garth Brooks' "The River". To me, that is what life is about; not knowing what life is going to bring you one day to the next.

In college, I had a roommate who listened to classical music, maybe because it helped him relax. I tried to listen to it, and then I tried again, but it just did not work for me. Classical music is like my lack of appreciation for a fine wine, the history and the culture are simply wasted on me. In years to come, I will learn to enjoy and truly appreciate the gift that classical music has to offer.

Music is one of the finest memory makers that I know. I can open my memory bank and think about all those concerts I have shared with family and friends. I can easily remember my last Nickleback concert; I took my sons, Josh and Brett. What was ironic about that concert was that one of the bands to headline Nickelback was Bush and it just so happens that the lead singer is Gavin Rossdale, who was married to Gwen Stefani at the time. At one point during the concert, Gavin was singing and moving through the crowd and he rubbed his hand across Josh's head, just like a father would do to a son. I guess I banged on her door and he answered. You never know what life is going to give you or where the music is going to take you.

Music Helps You Recharge

In our high-tech world, there are a number of applications that use music designed to relax you. Check out "OSI-Connect" or "PTSD Coach" and see what they have to offer. You do not have to have PTSD to appreciate what these applications can bring to your life. If they offer nothing to you, then suggest

Music can take you to a different place or a different time and help you to recharge your batteries.

them to someone else. Always remember that music can take you to a different place or a different time and help you to recharge your batteries. When you have chosen law enforcement as a practice, from time to time, you will have to do this just to keep a sense of who you are. Given the unique job pressures, it seems that police officers are a little bit more prone to becoming lost.

Once when Ray was over visiting, he shared a story of a time when he was trying to get a few things straight in his mind and stumbled across some music that helped put things in perspective. It is not so much what was happening but rather *how* he found the music that is the real story. He went out for a walk to clear his mind and found himself in front of a busker playing a cello. The next thing you know he was on the internet and came across these two guys, "2CELLOS". As an aside, you really have to hop online and see these guys at work.

On a funny note, when it comes to lyrics, how many times have you been driving down the road, singing along to your best loved song and find that the lyrics you are singing are not exactly the same as the artist's? Did you know that there is actually a website dedicated to misheard lyrics? When that happens to me, and there is someone in the car with me, I just tell them that is how I wrote it and the band decided to change the lyrics. If you subliminally change lyrics and the song ends up creating more meaning for you, who is to judge? Man, that reminds me of the Dan Hill lyrics, "... For who am I to judge you in what you say or do..."

"Earl Had to Die"

A particular song can surface at the most ironic time. There we were, just outside of beautiful Banff, Alberta, sitting on the hills not far from where a victim had been buried some years before. That particular homicide investigation unfolded like a Movie of the Week. In fact, a reporter later wrote a book about it based on the trial. It was called *Black Lies*. I am not sure whether art imitates life or vice versa, but as we sat there, the Dixie Chick's "Earl Had to Die" came on the radio. Now this victim was far from Earl, actually he was quite the opposite, but like the song, his wife decided that he had to die. He had to die, based on her twisted thoughts, but it is amazing to note the similarity in the storylines. Out of curiosity, I tried to determine when the music video came out as compared to this young man's death. My best guess is that the murder preceded the song. Nonetheless, you should have seen the looks on our faces when that song came on the radio.

I remember two distinct songs from the time that I was at Depot. The first one was by Bon Jovi and it was played at our halfway party. It is a bit of a cliché, but it still conjures up a memory when I hear the words "we're halfway there". The other song, which is more of a funny memory, is by the Righteous Brothers and was dedicated to our drill instructor. Drill was a class where you learned dress and deportment as well as discipline and teamwork. What you learned in drill class helped you when dealing with difficult clients in the field. Your instructor always came across as tough as nails, and if he did his job properly, he would make you shake in your boots. The expectation was clear: "Don't f--k it up" because, when you did, that meant push-ups. Somehow each troop developed a relationship with their drill corporal, and mine was no different. During our "Pass Out" (Graduation) we serenaded him with "You've Lost That Lovin' Feeling". I am not sure that it is still in his memory bank, but it was definitely our last hoorah with him.

Just the other night, I popped into a local bistro just to say hello to the bartender. As with a lot of bartenders, he convinced me to stay for a drink. Of course, I did, and on my way out, I stopped to speak to an old colleague. He asked me how my new job was going, and he told me that he had just finished taking a course. The course was one that I helped to develop, and I was quite proud of the product. It contained a number of case studies, and suddenly, there I was, speaking about investigations that I had touched. In short, I was living my own version of Springsteen's "Glory Days". I would have never pegged myself as a glory days kind of guy because I believe in living for tomorrow and believe that the past is the past.

Memories will always be ours, but life is about making new memories, whether they are planned or not. It is our memories that make the difference in our life. This always makes me think about the Alabama song "I am in a hurry (and don't know why)". The lyrics tell us that all we really have to do is live and die. The message is a very simple one, but more often than not, we lose focus. Music can help us remember what is truly important in life. That is why "Wayward Son" says so much to me. Dad was a big Alabama fan. He even saw them in concert. I still remember Dad telling the story of the lead singer falling flat on his ass up on the stage.

It was 2008, and Dad was losing his battle with cancer. I recall him saying that he did not think that he would go downhill so fast, and he began to blame himself, saying that he should have seen a doctor long before the cancer started taking over. There was a look of disappointment in his eye, as if he was letting everyone down. I told him not to be hard on himself because it really would not have made any difference because his cancer was genetically based. Anyone who has had a loved one attacked by cancer knows the feeling of helplessness in the pit of your stomach because you have absolutely no control over the situation. It is like being on a roller coaster ride; as you approach the top, you start having second thoughts, but you have no choice because you are already picking up speed and going down. I had planned a trip to Mexico with my daughters, and the time was getting near for the trip, but the time was also getting near for Dad. I had a heart to heart with Dad and told him that I was not going to take the trip. He was insistent that I not change my plans as he thought it was important for me to go and have fun with his granddaughters. This speaks volumes to the type of man Dad was. He was a friend to everyone, and he would give the shirt off his back for you. So, I took Nicole and Shantelle to Mexico. I called home every day and spoke to Mom, and she told me that Dad was hanging on. It was not an easy time. I knew Dad was in a lot of pain and that he would hang on until he could say goodbye to me.

Final Words

By the time the trip was over, Dad was declining rapidly. It was early in the morning – or the middle of the night depending on how you looked at it. I could not sleep and I wanted to see Dad but I knew that visiting hours were not in effect; however, this was not going to stop me. I went to the hospital and called up to the floor and the nurses let me in. The hospital was dark, and there was an uneasy kind of silence. I went into his room. Let me digress a little here. This room was a typical hospital room with four beds. This would be the place where Dad would spend his last precious moments in life, ushered into a stall like livestock. He was asleep, and I just sat there and watched him sleep.

This was my hero, my role model, and more recently, my friend, who was being ripped from his friends and family. He opened his eyes and the first thing he said was "What is wrong, Tom?" Even so near to the end, he was concerned about me and not himself. I just wanted to spend time with him. We did not have to speak to communicate with each other, and there was that constant sense of peace of simply being with Dad. I began to think, and in my heart, I knew that my time left with him on this earth would be short. What do you say to someone who has given you so much and still had so much more to give? I looked at Dad with all the tubes and machines hooked up to him and asked, "Do you have any advice?"

He knew what I was asking. I was not looking for advice on cars, women, or money; it was advice on life that I was seeking. He looked at me with his piercing hazel eyes and began to speak. It was an effort for him to speak; the cancer had been merciless with his body. He told me that sometimes I take on a little too much and mentioned some kind words about my daughters and how best to deal with those relationships. I would have loved to argue with him. He knew what the job was all about; he knew what the commitment was to the job. He knew how much passion I had for the job, but he was right. He was giving me sage advice and telling me to ensure that I had balance in my life. We all need balance. The level of balance required will be different for everyone, but it is

Some sense of balance is required if we are to remain healthy.

important to recognize that some sense of balance is required if we are to remain healthy.

It was in the early morning hours of September 1, 2008. When I awoke, I knew I had to go to the hospital. I struggled to get my clothes on and hopped in the van. I turned on the radio and heard these lyrics "...Carry on my wayward son, There'll be peace when you are done, Lay your weary head to rest, Don't you cry no more..."

I began to drive and did not get too far before my cell phone rang. It was my wife Janette telling me that Nicole was chasing after me. I turned the van around and picked up my daughter and together we went to the hospital. Dad had been moved to a private room, and Mom and my brother Chris were already there. We arrived just in time to see his last breaths.

Only be in a hurry to get things done when it matters to you and your family. If your head and heart are in the right place, when you hear a song on the radio that sparks a memory, then the fond memories will always outnumber the others.

Chapter Thirteen Sound Bites
- Music does make the world go around
- Music chooses us
- What are your theme songs?

EPILOGUE

It's all we've been given
So you better start livin' right now...
...Take 'em by the hand
Don't let 'em all fly by
Come on, Come on now
Don't you know the days go by

"Days Go By"
—Keith Urban, 2004

I am going to miss the people, but not the organization. Sounds like an old cliché, and then I begin to think about it. I am going to miss the organization just as much as the people. I spent my whole life with this organization, and it has given me stability and opportunities, but more importantly, it has allowed me to meet the people I will miss. I will miss them because of the memories and know I will not be able to create more of them in the organization. I would think that that is part of the challenge when making the decision to leave.

When people ask you who you are, do you tell them that you are a doctor, a lawyer, a policeman? I would venture most do, and we lose who we really are in this. I will always be Tom Caverly. This is important because you have to be comfortable in your own skin. Always stay grounded and know that one day you will have to move on to different things and leave that chapter behind you.

During my service, I have always paid particular attention when I hear what motivated the men and women I have worked with to join such an elite organization. As boys and girls, we all have dreams of what we are going to be when we grow up. For some, this comes naturally, and for others it takes some time to find their path. It really will depend on what you're looking for, what your passions are, or in some cases, simply being in the right place at the right time.

The Force is such a great environment for those diamonds in the rough waiting to be polished to a high shine. In my case, it was the love of my dad that set the wheels in motion for a fantastic career in law enforcement. While practicing law enforcement, I was able to meet interesting people and travel from one end of the country to the other and at times outside. I also had the opportunity to touch so many high profile investigations both locally and nationally. I influenced a South American country to advance its investigations using wiretap. If that is not exciting I am not quite sure what is. If that does not make you jump out of bed and say give me more I do not know what does.

It started with a question, "What are you going to be when you grow up?" I young but that is where my commitment began and eventually became a reality. Then there was my silent cheerleader along the way – Dad. If anything was to etch in stone that this would be my destiny it was Canada Day in our Nation's Capital in 1978. Dad's assignment for the day was red serge duty. There is nothing more awe inspiring then seeing a person wearing that uniform all polished up and bursting as a symbol of Canada.

This was my dad, and the way that the tourists were treating him was nothing less than a hero. They all wanted a picture with a Mountie. Throughout my service I have asked people why they have joined. I still remember and laugh at Stew's account. Stew grew up in Smith Falls, Ontario, and worked at a local psychiatric hospital with a couple of other guys, and one of these guys had his heart set on being a member. It turns out he was having some challenges going through the selection process. Each and every time he hit a wall, he would share the story with Stew. Stew finally had enough and bet the guy he could get hired. In no time, flat Stew was a Mountie and had a fantastic career also touching a number of high-profile investigations.

Then there was Murray, who was also from Ontario. He was listening to the radio and on comes this ad looking for people to join. Murray is still enjoying a great career in the RCMP in the commissioned ranks. Deanne will have similar memories as me. She too is second-generation Mountie (and her cousin is also a member). Darren is another story of a second-generation Mountie, but he told me such a touching story about how he told his dad that he was promoted to Sergeant Major. It brought tears to his dad's eyes he was so proud of his son. You cannot buy that kind of happiness. So it really is a family affair.

What about Linden? In conversations with Linden there was definitely some tension between him and his dad, but it was not over becoming a Mountie. You see Linden played pro football with the Hamilton Tiger Cats and actually played in a Grey Cup game. There have been plenty of pro athletes that have joined the Mounties, and they are a natural fit because being a police officer really is a team sport. Kevin grew up in P.E.I., and it was that one day he saw that Mountie knocking at the door that he met his calling, but not right away. He spent some time in the military and then joined the RCMP.

Finally there is Steve – one of the smartest people I have worked with. He had a passion to be a Mountie that would not die. It was not his original career choice. Steve's dad wanted great things for him. He wanted Steve to pursue a career practicing law. That

> **You need to have passion to do any job. It is in the passion that you will find your happy place and ultimate job satisfaction.**

is exactly what Steve did. He went to university, then law school and secured employment with a prominent law firm in the lower mainland.

I still remember him telling me how the RCMP recruiter was truly puzzled why Steve would give up such a luxurious office with a great view to join the Mounties. It was, and still is, Steve's passion. Steve's dad had a hard time with it until he actually saw his son on the job. He then realized that his son had met his calling. Steve has developed a successful skill set in major crime but currently serves in the capacity of a lawyer for the RCMP. At times, I was in awe of working with all of these people. They were all professionals who always showed up with their game face on, and I can honestly say that they have made a difference not only to the RCMP but also to the people of Canada.

I could go on with other people I have either worked with or come across with similar stories. I also got the feeling that the organization really did not appreciate these people for what they were worth. It is a group of individuals charged with passion, and if you dig down, and not too deep, you will find the true meaning of *esprit de corps*. The interesting thing about all of these people is that if you were to ask them if they really cared whether the RCMP truly showed them the appreciation they deserve, they would not care. It is not the reason they do these things. You cannot put a price on something that is priceless. If I had a dime for every time I said I was just like the wind – I wanted to be behind the scenes and help the best I could.

We, the collective we, are not looking for a pat on the back. We are Canadians answering a calling. A calling that will make a difference and a world of memories. It is a passion. You need to have passion to do any job. It is in the passion that you will find your happy place and ultimate job satisfaction. Find it wherever you want. It does not matter how you picked this profession; you will need the passion to survive. You may not realize what you have ever gotten yourself into, but it comes with understanding at one point. The understanding comes from knowing the job is reflective of a Canadian icon. You can say the same for anyone who enters a career in law enforcement. You want the same level of commitment.

How do you find your passion for this type of career? Well that is part of the journey. Like the people I have just spoken about, you will not have to dig too deep to find it. It does not matter if you are a member of the RCMP or any other force, you need to have esprit de corps. We all have it and are not afraid to show and share it and keep it alive from generation to generation. Esprit de corps will mean different things to different people, and we have an obligation to understand each other in that respect. A great starting point is just asking a colleague why they joined. Through this understanding esprit de corps will never become esprit de *corpse*.

No Rest for the Wicked... Even less for the Righteous!
(Inspired by Insp. Colin Thomson, Abbotsford Police Department)

TROOP DISMISSED!

Final Sound Bites
- Everyone has a story
- Find your passion or let your passion find you
- Have no regrets

APPENDIX A
RCMP MISSION, VISION AND VALUES

Mission

The RCMP is Canada's national police service. Proud of our traditions and confident in meeting future challenges, we commit to preserve the peace, uphold the law and provide quality service in partnership with our communities.

Vision

We will:

- Be a progressive, proactive and innovative organization;
- Provide the highest quality service through dynamic leadership, education and technology in partnership with the diverse communities we serve;
- Be accountable and efficient through shared decision-making;
- Ensure a healthy work environment that encourages team building, open communication and mutual respect;
- Promote safe communities;
- Demonstrate leadership in the pursuit of excellence.

Core Values of the RCMP

Recognizing the dedication of all employees, we will create and maintain an environment of individual safety, well-being and development. We are guided by:

- Integrity;
- Honesty;
- Professionalism;
- Compassion;
- Respect;
- Accountability.

Commitment to Our Communities

The employees of the RCMP are committed to our communities through:

- Unbiased and respectful treatment of all people;
- Accountability;
- Mutual problem solving;
- Cultural sensitivity;
- Enhancement of public safety;
- Partnerships and consultation;
- Open and honest communication;
- Effective and efficient use of resources;
- Quality and timely service.

Commitment to the Employees of the RCMP

Commitment to the employees of the RCMP – In the spirit of shared leadership and recognizing all employees as our greatest asset, we commit to:

- Open, honest and bilateral communication;
- Demonstrating leadership through accountability and responsibility at all levels;
- Treating all employees with equal respect and consideration;
- Ensuring the safety of our employees by developing and enforcing minimum resourcing standards;
- Training that is timely, specific to the needs and relevant to job requirements
- Effective and efficient management of human resources through consultation, teamwork and empowerment at all levels;
- Ensuring a safe and harassment free work environment;
- Encouraging and recognizing innovation and creativity;

Implementing fair and equitable systems to address:

- Recognition for good performers;
- Compensation and entitlements;
- Financial hardship caused by employees' worksite;
- Consistently poor performers;
- Discipline and discharge;
- Promoting health, safety and well-being;
- Ensuring adequate human, financial and material resources;
- Enhancing job security through marketing of our services.

The RCMP's mission, vision and value statement was created in the fall of 1995 as a result of an initiative led by, then Commissioner, Joseph Philip Robert Murray.

Printed in Canada